YOUR re̶ W9-CFX-323
could appear
in our next
cookbook!

Share your tried & true family favorites with us instantly at

www.gooseberrypatch.com

If you'd rather jot 'em down by hand, just mail this form to...
Gooseberry Patch • Cookbooks – Call for Recipes
2500 Farmers Dr., #110 • Columbus, OH 43235

If your recipe is selected for a book, you'll receive a FREE copy!

Please share only your original recipes or those that you have made your own over the years.

Recipe Name:

Number of Servings:

Any fond memories about this recipe? Special touches you like to add
or handy shortcuts?

Ingredients (include specific measurements):

Instructions (continue on back if needed):

Special Code: **cookbookspage**

Over ↗

Extra space for recipe if needed:

Tell us about yourself...

Your complete contact information is needed so that we can send you your FREE cookbook, if your recipe is published. Phone numbers and email addresses are kept private and will only be used if we have questions about your recipe.

Name:
Address:
City: State: Zip:
Email:
Daytime Phone:

Thank you! Vickie & Jo Ann

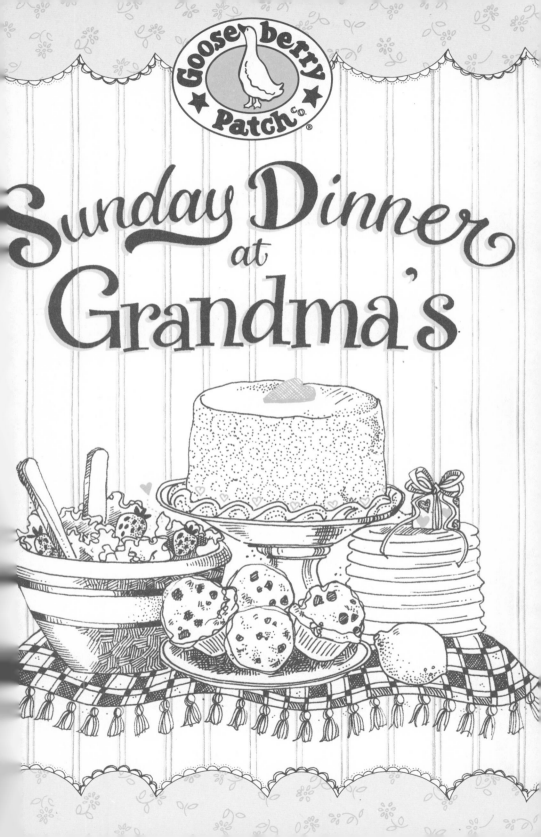

Sunday Dinner at Grandma's

Gooseberry Patch
2500 Farmers Dr., #110
Columbus, OH 43235

www.gooseberrypatch.com

1·800·854·6673

Copyright 2010, Gooseberry Patch 978-1-936283-04-0
Third Printing, February, 2011

Do you have a tried & true recipe...

tip, craft or memory that you'd like to see featured in a **Gooseberry
Patch** cookbook? Visit our website at **www.gooseberrypatch.com**
to share them with us instantly. If you'd rather jot them down by hand,
use the handy form in the front of this book and send them to...

Gooseberry Patch
Attn: Cookbook Dept.
2500 Farmers Dr., #110
Columbus, OH 43235

Don't forget to include the number of servings your recipe makes,
plus your name, address, phone number and email address.
If we select your recipe, your name will appear right along
with it...and you'll receive a **FREE** copy of the cookbook!

Contents

Dedication

To everyone with fond
memories of family, food
and Sunday dinner
at Grandma's.

Appreciation

To all of you who
opened up your
recipe boxes and your
hearts...thanks!

RISE & SHINE
Breakfasts

Amish Breakfast Casserole

Barb Bargdill
Gooseberry Patch

I liked to make this hearty dish when my boys came home from college for the holidays. My mom, their grandmother, used to make it when my brothers, sisters and I came home to visit too, so I got the recipe from her and carried on the tradition.

1 lb. bacon, diced
1 sweet onion, chopped
1 green pepper, diced
10 eggs, beaten
1-1/2 c. cream-style cottage
  cheese

4 c. frozen shredded
  hashbrowns, thawed
2 c. shredded Cheddar cheese
1-1/2 c. shredded Monterey Jack
  cheese, divided

In a large skillet over medium heat, cook bacon, onion and green pepper until bacon is crisp; drain and set aside. In a large bowl, combine remaining ingredients, reserving 1/4 cup of the Monterey Jack cheese. Stir bacon mixture into egg mixture. Transfer to a greased 13"x9" baking pan; sprinkle with reserved cheese. Bake, uncovered, at 350 degrees for 35 to 40 minutes, until set and bubbly. Let stand 10 minutes before cutting. Makes 8 to 10 servings.

A well-loved china teapot that's been handed down to you makes a sweet vase for garden roses, daffodils or daisies.

Overnight Breakfast Casserole

Kelly Patrick
Ashburn, VA

*My Aunt Linda served this recipe to my family when we visited her out
in California. We've been making it for over twenty years now for
ourselves, for friends and even for brunch meetings at work. It's a sure
winner...and so easy to make!*

1/4 loaf sourdough bread, cubed
2 c. shredded Cheddar cheese
16-oz. pkg. ground pork
   sausage, browned and
   drained
4 eggs, beaten

3 c. milk
10-3/4 oz. can cream of
   mushroom soup
4-oz. can diced green chiles
3/4 t. dry mustard
1/8 t. chili powder

Place bread in a lightly greased 13"x9" baking pan; top with cheese
and sausage. Whisk together remaining ingredients and pour over
top. Cover with aluminum foil; refrigerate overnight. Let stand for
30 minutes before baking. Bake, uncovered, at 350 degrees for
one hour, or until set in the middle. Serves 8.

Sunday morning is often busy, so why not get the day off to
a great start? Put together a make-ahead breakfast casserole
and refrigerate. The next day, pop it in the oven for a hot,
hearty breakfast with no fuss at all!

Stir-Abouts

Rebekah Caillouet
West Milton, OH

A special breakfast treat my Great-Grandma Heckaman always made for us when we stayed overnight with her. It's quite an old recipe that's something like a pancake.

2 c. all-purpose flour
1 T. sugar
2 t. baking powder
1/2 t. salt

2 c. milk
1 egg, beaten
Garnish: butter, maple syrup

In a large bowl, beat all ingredients except garnish together until smooth. Heat a lightly greased skillet over medium-high heat. Drop large spoonfuls of the batter into skillet. When golden on one side, turn over with a pancake turner; chop batter into one-inch pieces. Keep turning and cooking until set and golden on all sides. Serve with butter and maple syrup. Serves 4.

Making stacks of pancakes for a crowd? Keep them warm and yummy...just arrange pancakes on a baking sheet, set in a 200-degree oven, then serve as needed.

Grandmom's Corn Fritters

Lisa Ann Panzino DiNunzio
Vineland, NJ

Ever since I was a child, my grandmother would serve up huge plates full of these yummy fritters. We would dig in eagerly and they were gone in no time! Grandmom's in her late eighties now and still makes them for us from time to time.

15-1/4 oz. can corn
14-3/4 oz. can creamed corn
1/4 c. milk
3 eggs, beaten

1/4 t. salt
1-2/3 c. all-purpose flour
oil for frying
Optional: jam or apple butter

In a large bowl, mix together corn with liquid, creamed corn, milk, eggs and salt. Stir in flour, a little at a time, to make a pancake batter consistency. Add a little more flour if mixture is too wet. Add oil generously to a large skillet over medium-high heat. Drop batter mixture onto the skillet by heaping tablespoonfuls. Fry on both sides until lightly golden. Drain fritters on a paper towel-lined platter. Serve warm, plain or garnished as desired. Makes about 15.

Berry Butter

Laura Fuller
Fort Wayne, IN

Try this yummy fruit butter with strawberries too!

1/2 c. butter, softened
1/3 c. raspberries

2 T. powdered sugar
1/8 t. lemon juice

Combine all ingredients in a small bowl; blend well. Serve immediately or chill until using. Makes about 3/4 cup.

Overstuffed French Toast

Jessica Silva
East Berlin, CT

One of my family's favorite breakfast recipes. The idea came from a well-known restaurant chain...I tried their version and thought I could make it even better at home. I think I succeeded!

8-oz. pkg. cream cheese,
  softened
1/2 c. butter, softened
1-1/4 t. vanilla extract, divided
3/4 c. powdered sugar
2 T. brown sugar, packed

3 eggs, beaten
1 t. maple syrup
cinnamon to taste
8 thick slices bread
butter for frying

With an electric mixer on low speed, beat cream cheese and butter until well blended. Beat in 1/4 teaspoon vanilla and sugars; set aside. Combine eggs, remaining vanilla and maple syrup in a shallow bowl. Whisk until well blended. Sprinkle cinnamon over mixture. Heat a griddle over medium heat. Place bread in egg mixture, one slice at a time, until first side is moistened; flip and moisten the second side. Melt a pat of butter on griddle; add bread slices and cook until golden on both sides. For each serving, place one toast slice on a plate and spoon cream cheese mixture on top. Top with second toast slice and warm Berry Topping. Serves 4.

Berry Topping:

10-oz. pkg. frozen berries
1/4 c. sugar

1 T. maple syrup or
  berry-flavored syrup

In a saucepan over medium-low heat, combine berries, sugar and syrup. Heat through, stirring until sugar dissolves; keep warm.

Set aside day-old bread for making French toast...it absorbs the milk better than bakery-fresh bread. A thrifty tip that's tasty too.

Good Morning Monkey Bread

Faith Colopy
Katy, TX

This recipe has been sweetly handed down by my grandmother...her memory lives on as I share in one of her greatest gifts, cooking! When I bake this overnight sensation, we all remember Grams.

18 frozen white dinner rolls
3/4 c. sugar
3/4 c. brown sugar, packed
3-1/2 oz. pkg. cook & serve
   butterscotch pudding mix

3 to 4 t. cinnamon
1/2 c. butter, sliced
Optional: 1/2 c. chopped pecans

Scatter frozen rolls in a Bundt® pan that has been sprayed with non-stick vegetable spray. Rolls will expand, so take care not to overfill pan. Set aside. In a separate bowl, mix sugars, dry pudding mix and cinnamon together. Sprinkle mixture on top of frozen rolls; dot with butter. Cover pan with a tea towel; let rise overnight. In the morning, uncover and bake at 350 degrees for 30 to 45 minutes. Remove from oven and let stand 15 to 20 minutes. Turn pan over onto a serving tray; spoon warm syrup from pan over bread. Makes 1-1/2 dozen rolls.

If it's a beautiful day, carry breakfast outdoors! Spread out a homespun quilt on the picnic table and enjoy the fresh air and early-morning sunshine.

Best-Ever Brunch Casserole

Andrea Galgon
Allentown, PA

I remember growing up with this as our Sunday morning brunch.
I would always help Mom by lining the pan with the bread.

6 slices bread
1 to 2 T. butter, softened
1 to 1-1/2 lbs. ground pork
   sausage, browned and
   drained
6 eggs, beaten

2 c. milk
1 t. mustard
1 t. salt
1 t. pepper
1 c. shredded Cheddar cheese

Spread bread slices with butter; cut bread into cubes. Line the bottom
of a lightly greased 13"x9" baking pan with bread cubes. Sprinkle
sausage over bread. Combine other ingredients and mix well; pour
over top. Bake, uncovered, at 350 degrees for 40 to 50 minutes.
Serves 4 to 6.

Hearty Farm Breakfast

Tonya Adams
Magnolia, KY

My grandma used to serve this to the farmhands who worked on our
family farm. It's especially scrumptious served on buttered toast.

4 slices bacon, chopped
1 T. onion, chopped
3 potatoes, peeled, boiled and
   diced
1/2 tomato, chopped

1/2 t. salt
1/4 to 1/2 t. pepper
5 eggs, beaten
1/2 c. American cheese, chopped

In a skillet over medium-high heat, sauté bacon. Drain, reserving one
tablespoon drippings in skillet. Add vegetables, salt and pepper. Sauté
until potatoes start to turn golden. Add eggs and cheese; cook and stir
over low heat until eggs are set. Serves 4.

Abuela's Garlic Grits

Kelly Petty
Aiken, SC

My grandmother's most-requested recipe. Her name was Frances, but my daughter lovingly called her Abuela (Spanish for grandmother) because she was a Spanish professor.

4-1/2 c. water
1 t. salt
1 c. quick-cooking grits, uncooked
1/2 c. butter, cubed
3/4 lb. pasteurized process cheese spread, cubed

2 eggs, beaten
2/3 c. milk
1/4 t. garlic powder
1 c. wheat & barley cereal nuggets
hot pepper sauce to taste

In a saucepan over high heat, bring water and salt to a boil. Slowly stir in grits; cook 3 to 5 minutes, stirring constantly. Remove from heat. Add butter and cheese, stirring until melted. Beat eggs, milk and garlic powder together; stir into hot mixture. Pour into an ungreased 13"x9" glass baking pan. Sprinkle with cereal and hot sauce. Bake, uncovered, at 350 degrees for one hour. Let stand 15 minutes before serving. Serves 10 to 12.

Indulge in an old farmhouse tradition...a big slice of apple or cherry pie for breakfast!

Apple Orchard Muffins

Tracey Ten Eyck
Austin, TX

This recipe was given to me by my Granny Mann when I first began learning to bake. She was the closest I had to a grandparent growing up, since both sets of grandparents lived out of town.

1 c. sugar
1/3 c. shortening
1 egg, beaten
1/4 c. milk
1 t. vanilla extract
1-1/2 c. all-purpose flour

1 t. baking soda
1 t. salt
2 c. apples, cored, peeled and
    chopped
Garnish: additional sugar

Blend sugar and shortening in a large bowl; stir in egg, milk and vanilla. Sift in flour, baking soda and salt; mix well. Stir in apples. Fill greased muffin cups 2/3 full; sprinkle tops of muffins with sugar. Bake at 375 degrees for 25 minutes. Makes one dozen.

The taste of fresh-baked muffins, anytime! Place cooled muffins in a freezer bag and freeze. To serve, wrap individual muffins in aluminum foil and pop into a 300-degree oven for a few minutes, until toasty warm.

Raspberry Cream Muffins

Cathy Elgin
Saint Louis Park, MN

*My husband loves these muffins! We use fresh berries from
our own raspberry bushes.*

1 c. raspberries
3/4 c. plus 2 T. sugar, divided
1/4 c. butter, softened
1 egg, beaten
1 t. almond extract
2-1/4 c. all-purpose flour

1 T. baking powder
1/2 t. salt
1 c. half-and-half
1 c. white chocolate chips,
   finely chopped
2 T. brown sugar, packed

In a small bowl, toss raspberries with 1/4 cup sugar; set aside. In a
large bowl, blend butter and 1/2 cup sugar. Beat in egg and extract.
Combine flour, baking powder and salt; add to butter mixture
alternately with half-and-half. Stir in raspberries and chocolate chips.
Fill paper-lined muffin cups 2/3 full. Combine brown sugar and
remaining sugar; sprinkle over batter. Bake at 350 degrees for 25 to
30 minutes. Cool for 5 minutes before removing muffins to a wire
rack. Serve warm. Makes one dozen.

Lemon Butter Spread

Gloria Costes
West Hills, CA

*My grandmother, who was a great cook, brought this recipe with her
from England. Real butter makes it irresistible. I enjoy it on toast and
muffins...even on angel food cake or over ice cream.*

1 c. butter
2 c. sugar
2 eggs, beaten

1/2 c. lemon juice
1 T. lemon zest

In the top of a double boiler over boiling water, melt butter. Stir in
remaining ingredients. Cook, uncovered, over simmering water for
one hour, or until thickened, stirring occasionally. Pour into airtight
containers; cover and store in refrigerator. Makes 3 cups.

Peanut Butter Cake

Jennifer Bryant
Bowling Green, KY

This recipe comes to me by way of my Ol' Nanny. It is definitely a family favorite even at breakfast time...dense, moist and even better the next day!

2 c. self-rising flour
2 c. sugar
1/2 c. milk
2 eggs, beaten

1 t. vanilla extract
1 c. margarine, melted
1 c. cold water
1 c. creamy peanut butter

Combine flour and sugar in a large bowl. Add milk, eggs and vanilla; stir well. Mix margarine, water and peanut butter. Add to flour mixture; blend until smooth. Spread in a greased 13"x9" baking pan. Bake at 350 degrees for 35 to 40 minutes. Spread Frosting on cooled cake. Makes 12 servings.

Frosting:

16-oz. pkg. powdered sugar
1/2 c. margarine, melted

1/4 c. milk
1/2 c. creamy peanut butter

Combine all ingredients and mix well.

No self-rising flour in the pantry? Try this! To equal one cup self-rising flour, substitute one cup all-purpose flour plus 1-1/2 teaspoons baking powder and 1/2 teaspoon salt.

Pecan Coffee Cake

Kelly Patrick
Ashburn, VA

Mom taught me how to make my dad's favorite coffee cake when I was young. I was always an early riser, and I started to get up extra early on Sunday mornings just to make coffee cake for Dad before he woke up. It always brings back wonderful memories!

1-1/2 c. butter, softened and
    divided
1 c. sugar
2 eggs, beaten
1 t. vanilla extract

3 c. all-purpose flour
1 T. baking powder
1/2 t. salt
1 c. milk

Blend one cup butter and sugar in a large bowl. Stir in eggs and vanilla; set aside. Mix flour, baking powder and salt in a separate bowl. Add flour mixture and milk alternately to butter mixture; stir well. Pour half of batter into a lightly greased and floured 13"x9" baking pan. Sprinkle half of Pecan Filling over batter. Top with remaining batter, then remaining filling. Melt remaining butter; drizzle over top. Bake at 375 degrees for 20 to 30 minutes. Serves 8 to 12.

Pecan Filling:

1-1/2 c. brown sugar, packed
2 t. cinnamon

1 c. broken pecans

Mix together in a small bowl.

Such sweet placecards...tie a ribbon around each guest's juice glass and tuck in a tiny childhood snapshot.

Iva's Cinnamon Rolls

Bobbi Janssen
Lanark, IL

When I first met my husband's Grandma Iva, she instantly accepted me as her own granddaughter! She showed me how to make these yummy cinnamon rolls. I have learned that anyone can pass on a recipe, but to watch how a recipe is artfully put together is priceless.

1 t. active dry yeast
3 c. very warm water, divided
1 c. lard or shortening
2 eggs, beaten
1 c. sugar

1 T. salt
8 c. all-purpose flour
1/4 c. butter, softened
1/2 c. brown sugar, packed
1 T. cinnamon

Dissolve yeast in a tablespoon of very warm water, 110 to 115 degrees. In a separate bowl, add lard or shortening to remaining water; set aside. Mix together eggs, sugar and salt. In a large bowl, combine yeast mixture, lard mixture and egg mixture; stir in flour. Turn dough into a greased bowl; cover with a tea towel. Let rise for 5 hours; punch down dough every hour. Divide dough into 2 parts. Roll each part into an 18-inch by 13-inch rectangle. Spread butter over surface. Sprinkle with brown sugar and cinnamon, adding more to taste if desired. Roll up, starting on one long side; cut into one-inch thick slices. Place into 2 greased 10" round baking pans. Cover; let rise for several hours to overnight, until double in size. Bake at 350 degrees for about 20 minutes. Cool and spread with Frosting. Makes 2-1/2 dozen.

Frosting:

4 c. powdered sugar
1/4 c. butter, softened

1 T. to 1/4 c. milk

Combine powdered sugar and butter; add milk to desired consistency.

Stitch a few whimsical charms, buttons or beads around the edges of a tea cozy, to bring a smile every morning.

Honey Bun Cake

Trish Gothard
York, PA

Whenever this yummy cake is baking, the spicy smell reminds me of my mom making cinnamon toast for us on very cold mornings.

18-1/2 oz. pkg. yellow cake mix
8-oz. container sour cream
4 eggs, beaten
2/3 c. oil
1/3 c. water
1/2 c. brown sugar, packed
1 t. cinnamon

Combine dry cake mix, sour cream, eggs, oil and water in a large bowl. Beat with an electric mixer on medium speed until smooth. In a separate bowl, mix brown sugar and cinnamon. Pour half of cake batter into a greased and floured 13"x9" baking pan; sprinkle half of brown sugar mixture over batter. Repeat layers; gently swirl with a table knife. Bake at 350 degrees for 25 minutes. Drizzle Powdered Sugar Glaze over warm cake; cut into squares. Makes 24 servings.

Powdered Sugar Glaze:

1 c. powdered sugar
1/2 t. vanilla extract
2 t. milk

Stir together ingredients to make a glaze consistency.

What good fortune to grow up in a home where there are grandparents.

-Suzanne LaFollette

Mashed Potato Doughnuts

Shaunda Brown
Fairborn, OH

This recipe has been in our family for at least two generations. I can remember everyone coming to my grandma's house to help make doughnuts...a doughnut party, what fun!

2 eggs, beaten
2 c. sugar
2 c. mashed potatoes
3 T. butter, melted
1 c. milk
4 t. baking powder

1/2 t. baking soda
2 t. nutmeg
1 t. salt
5 c. all-purpose flour
oil for deep frying

Mix eggs, sugar, mashed potatoes and butter in a large bowl. Stir in remaining ingredients except oil; mix well. Roll out dough 1/2-inch thick and cut with a doughnut cutter. In a deep fryer, heat several inches of oil to 400 degrees. Add doughnuts, a few at a time; fry for 2 to 3 minutes, until golden. Drain on paper towels. Makes about 2 dozen.

Turn a tag-sale picture frame into a charming tea tray. Remove the glass and paint the frame, if you like. Then arrange family photos, vintage greeting cards and handwritten recipes under the glass.

Easy Chocolate Doughnuts

Sarah McCone
Eaton Rapids, MI

My mother-in-law makes these doughnuts at family gatherings.
Sometimes instead of frosting them, we just toss them in
cinnamon-sugar. Either way, you'll love them like we do.

16.3-oz. tube refrigerated
  biscuits

shortening for deep frying

Separate and flatten biscuits, or use a small cutter to cut out a hole in
the center without flattening. In a frying pan over medium-high heat,
heat one inch of shortening to 375 degrees. Add biscuits, several at a
time; cook until golden, one to 2 minutes on each side. Drain on paper
towels; frost with Chocolate Frosting. Makes 8.

Chocolate Frosting:

2 c. powdered sugar
1 T. baking cocoa

1 to 2 t. water

Mix ingredients together. Stir to desired consistency, adding a little
more water if needed.

Invite your sisters and best girlfriends over for brunch! Share
coffee cake, small talk and a quick craft...lavender sachets to tuck
into linen closets. Add a scoop of dried lavender to the center of a
vintage flowered hankie, gather it up and tie with a pretty ribbon.

Mile-High Buttermilk Biscuits

Staci Meyers
Montezuma, GA

My secret? Use a sharp biscuit cutter and don't twist it when cutting out your biscuits...you'll be amazed how high they rise!

2 c. all-purpose flour
1 T. baking powder
1 t. salt
1/2 c. lard or shortening, chilled
    in freezer

2/3 to 3/4 c. buttermilk
1/4 c. butter, melted

Mix together flour, baking powder and salt. Cut in lard or shortening until a crumbly texture is reached. Stir in buttermilk until incorporated and dough leaves sides of bowl. Dough will be sticky. Knead dough 3 to 4 times on a lightly floured surface. Roll out to 1/2-inch thickness, about 2 to 4 passes with a rolling pin. Cut dough with a biscuit cutter, pressing straight down with cutter. Place biscuits on a parchment paper-lined baking sheet. Bake at 500 degrees for 8 to 10 minutes. Brush tops of warm biscuits with melted butter. Makes about one dozen.

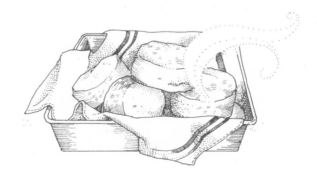

For the flakiest biscuits, just stir to moisten and gently roll or pat the dough...don't overmix it.

Sawmill Sausage Gravy

Gretchen Phillips
Redkey, IN

This recipe has been handed down from my mother. It's delicious spooned over fresh-baked biscuits.

1 lb. ground pork sausage,
  formed into patties
2 T. all-purpose flour

1-1/2 c. milk
salt and pepper to taste

In a skillet over medium heat, brown sausage patties. Remove patties to drain on paper towels, reserving drippings in skillet. Add flour to reserved drippings and stir until browned. Slowly whisk in milk; cook and stir until smooth and thickened. Thin with hot water, if needed. Crumble sausage patties into gravy; season with salt and pepper. Makes 3 cups.

Chocolatey Cocoa Gravy

Linda Rhoades
Gardendale, AL

Ladle this over hot buttered biscuits...it is great! I first ate this at my grandmother's house and it became a family favorite. Use heaping tablespoonfuls of flour and cocoa.

1 c. sugar
2 c. water

1 T. all-purpose flour
1 T. baking cocoa

Mix all ingredients together in a saucepan. Cook and stir over medium heat until thickened. Makes 3 cups.

Use a mini slow cooker set on low to keep sweet or savory gravy piping-hot at breakfast.

Zucchini Pancakes

Nancy Dearbern
Erie, PA

You'll love these tender pancakes...they're super for a brunch buffet!

1/2 c. biscuit baking mix
1/4 c. grated Parmesan cheese
salt and pepper to taste
2 eggs, beaten

2 c. zucchini, shredded
oil for frying
Garnish: butter, maple syrup,
   sour cream

Combine all ingredients except oil and garnish; stir until mixed. Heat oil in a skillet over medium-high heat. Drop batter by 2 tablespoonfuls into skillet. Cook until golden on both sides. Serve warm, garnished as desired. Makes 4 servings.

Sweet Honey Butter

Lynn Williams
Muncie, IN

Grandma used to spoil us by stirring up this yummy spread whenever she served waffles or muffins.

1/2 c. butter, softened
1/4 c. powdered sugar

1/4 c. honey
1 t. vanilla extract

Blend butter and powdered sugar together until smooth. Add honey and vanilla; mix well. Store in a small covered container. Makes about 3/4 cup.

Whip up some fun-shaped pancakes for the kids! Lightly coat the inside of a cookie cutter with non-stick vegetable spray, then secure a clip clothespin to the side for easy turning. Set in a skillet and pour in the pancake batter.

Grandma's Waffle Spice Cakes

Suzanne Bayorgeon
Norfolk, NY

My grandmother could whip up a batch of her waffles without measuring a thing! Try them...they're delicious and your house will smell wonderful while they're baking.

1 T. shortening
1 egg, beaten
1/2 c. milk
1 c. brown sugar, packed
1-1/2 c. all-purpose flour
2 t. baking powder

1/4 t. salt
1 t. cinnamon
1 t. allspice
1 t. ground cloves
Garnish: butter, maple syrup

Mix together shortening, egg and milk in a large bowl. Gradually stir in remaining ingredients except garnish. Ladle batter into an oiled waffle iron. Bake according to manufacturer's instructions. Serve with butter and maple syrup. Makes 4 servings.

Garden-fresh strawberries, blueberries and peaches are luscious on waffles and pancakes. Frozen fruit is yummy too and available year 'round...simmer fruit with a little sugar until it's syrupy. What a scrumptious way to start the day!

Upside-Down Eggs & Potatoes

Jessica Dekoekkoek
Richmond, VA

My husband's favorite Sunday breakfast! It always makes an impressive presentation yet is deceptively simple to prepare.

2 to 3 T. olive oil
1 to 2 potatoes, shredded
1-1/2 t. garlic powder
1-1/2 t. onion powder
1/2 t. paprika

1-1/2 c. shredded Mexican-
  blend cheese
6 eggs
salt and pepper to taste
Garnish: sour cream, salsa

Heat oil in a deep 12" oven-proof skillet over medium heat. Pat potatoes dry; add seasonings and toss to mix. Add potatoes to skillet. When about half cooked, use the back of a wooden spoon to smooth out potatoes over the bottom and up the sides of the skillet, to form a crust with no holes. Add cheese in an even layer. Beat eggs very well; add salt and pepper to taste. Gently pour in eggs over cheese. Bake, uncovered, at 375 degrees for 25 to 35 minutes, until a knife tip comes out clean. Carefully unmold onto a serving plate. Let stand for 10 minutes before cutting into wedges. Serve with sour cream and salsa. Makes 6 servings.

A cast-iron skillet is perfect for cooking up hashbrowns with the crispest golden crust. If the skillet hasn't been used in awhile, season it first...rub it all over with oil and bake at 300 degrees for an hour. Cool completely before removing from the oven.

Crispy Potato Pancakes

Mary Lou Thomas
Portland, ME

Tasty alongside scrambled eggs and bacon.

4 c. frozen shredded
   hashbrowns, thawed
1/2 c. onion, finely chopped
1/4 c. fresh parsley, minced
2 T. milk

2 eggs, beaten
1/4 c. all-purpose flour
1 t. salt
oil for frying

Combine all ingredients except oil; mix well. In a skillet over medium-high heat, heat 1/4-inch oil. Drop potato mixture by 1/4 cupfuls into hot oil. Fry until golden on both sides. Drain on paper towels. Serves 4.

Poached eggs are delicious atop corned beef hash. Add 2 inches of water and a tablespoon of white vinegar to a skillet. Bring to a simmer over high heat. Break an egg into a teacup and slide it into the water; add up to 3 more eggs. Simmer for 3 to 5 minutes, until as firm as you like. Serve eggs with a slotted spoon.

Grammie's Coffee Cake

Amy Stoltz
Saybrook, IL

This is a very special recipe to my four sisters and me. Grammie, who was my father's mother, was an exceptional cook and showed her love for us through her cooking.

1/2 c. shortening
1 egg, beaten
1-3/4 c. sugar, divided
2 c. all-purpose flour
1 t. baking powder
1 t. baking soda

1 c. buttermilk
Optional: raisins, dried fruit, candied cherries, chopped nuts, flaked coconut
2 t. cinnamon
1/2 c. margarine, melted

Combine shortening, egg and one cup sugar in a large bowl; beat with an electric mixer on medium speed. Sift together flour, baking powder and baking soda; add to shortening mixture along with buttermilk. Beat until well mixed; pour into a greased 13"x9" baking pan. Top with optional ingredients, as desired. Mix together remaining sugar and cinnamon; sprinkle over batter. Drizzle melted margarine over top. Bake at 350 degrees for 30 to 35 minutes. Serve warm. Makes 2 dozen servings.

Fresh-squeezed orange juice is always a treat. Set out an old-fashioned juicer along with a big bowl of halved oranges, so guests can take a turn at squeezing their own.

Snickerdoodle Scones

Charmie Fisher
Fontana, CA

Such yummy scones! I created this recipe because of my husband's love of the snickerdoodle cookies his grandma used to make. These scones are a new twist that bring back pleasant memories for him.

1/2 c. sour cream
1/2 t. baking soda
2 c. all-purpose flour
1/2 c. sugar
1 t. baking powder
1/8 t. cream of tartar
1/2 t. salt
1/2 c. butter
1 egg, beaten
2 t. cinnamon
Garnish: additional sugar and cinnamon

Combine sour cream and baking soda in a small bowl; set aside. Combine flour, sugar, baking powder, cream of tartar and salt. Cut in butter until mixture resembles fine bread crumbs. Whisk egg and cinnamon into sour cream mixture; add to flour mixture and stir until just moistened. Gather dough into a ball and place on a baking sheet sprayed with non-stick vegetable spray. Pat into a circle, 3/4-inch thick. Cut into 8 wedges and separate slightly on baking sheet. Dust with sugar and cinnamon. Bake at 350 degrees for 15 to 20 minutes, until golden. Makes 8 scones.

Invite the new neighbors or the new family at church over for brunch. Send them home with a basket of fresh-baked goodies wrapped in a tea towel...what a friendly gesture!

Whole-Wheat Pancakes

Katie Cooper
Chubbuck, ID

My grandparents were famous for these pancakes at the Wagon Wheel Motel they owned. Every Saturday in the summer they would make an enormous batch of pancakes and feed all their guests. I grew up eating them too...they are very filling and the best! Be sure to use whole-grain wheat, not whole-wheat flour.

3/4 c. whole-grain wheat	1 t. baking soda
1 c. milk	2 eggs, beaten
2 T. sugar	1/2 c. oil
1/4 t. salt	oil for frying
2 t. baking powder	

In a blender, mix whole wheat and milk. Blend on low speed for 4 minutes. While continuing to blend, add remaining ingredients except oil for frying. Heat a small amount of oil in a skillet over medium-high heat. Drop batter by 1/4 cupfuls into skillet. Cook until golden on both sides. Serves 4.

Homemade Buttery Syrup

Susan Matlock
Mansfield, MO

When I was growing up, my favorite breakfast was at my girlfriend's house...I'm now a part of that family! Her mother always fixed us chocolate pancakes and this yummy syrup, made from an old family recipe passed down by at least four generations.

2 c. sugar	1 t. vanilla extract
1 c. evaporated milk	3 T. butter

Combine sugar and evaporated milk in a saucepan over medium heat. Bring to a boil; reduce heat to low and simmer 10 minutes. Watch carefully to avoid scorching. Remove from heat; add vanilla and butter. Serve warm. Makes about 3 cups.

Welsh Rabbit

Geneva Rogers
Gillette, WY

Mmm...cheese sauce on toast! On chilly days, my brother and I used to beg my grandmother to make this dish for us...I think we liked the name as much as anything, but it really is good.

2 T. butter
16-oz. pkg. shredded sharp
   Cheddar cheese
2 eggs, beaten
1/2 c. beer or chicken broth

1/2 t. salt
1/2 t. dry mustard
1/8 t. cayenne pepper
1 t. Worcestershire sauce
8 slices bread, toasted

Place the top pan of a double boiler directly over medium-low heat; add butter and melt. Add cheese and cook, stirring occasionally, until cheese is melted. Set pan over boiling water in bottom of double boiler. Whisk together remaining ingredients except toast; add to cheese mixture. Cook until thickened, stirring frequently. To serve, spoon hot cheese mixture over toast. Makes 8 servings.

Add the nutty taste of whole grains to breakfast...they're delicious and healthy too! Try toasted whole-wheat bread, multigrain English muffins and pancakes with a sprinkle of wheat germ stirred into the batter.

Chili Egg Puff

Jean Stoner
New York, NY

Slice this spicy dish into smaller squares to serve as
a zesty appetizer at your brunch buffet.

10 eggs
1/2 c. all-purpose flour
1/2 t. baking powder
1/2 t. salt
16-oz. pkg. shredded Monterey
    Jack cheese

16-oz. container cottage cheese
1/2 c. butter, melted
7-oz. can diced green chiles

In a large bowl, beat eggs with an electric mixer on medium speed until light and lemon-colored. Add remaining ingredients except chiles; blend until smooth. Stir in chiles. Pour mixture into a well-buttered 13"x9" baking pan. Bake, uncovered, at 350 degrees for 45 minutes, or until top is golden and center is firm. Cut into squares to serve. Makes 8 to 10 servings.

Keep both early risers and sleepyheads happy with fresh, hot breakfasts...it's simple. Fill individual ramekins or custard cups with a favorite breakfast casserole and bake as needed.

Monte Christian Sandwiches

Michele Edmonds
Red Hook, NY

*While camping with our son, Christian, we asked him what he wanted for breakfast the next day. He thought about the breakfast items we had brought with us and came up with these sandwiches. They tasted so good I told him I would send the recipe to **Gooseberry Patch**, and here it is!*

1 T. butter, divided
4 eggs, divided
1/4 c. milk
4 slices bread

Optional: 2 slices favorite cheese
2 pork sausage breakfast
　　patties, browned and drained
Optional: maple syrup

In a skillet over medium heat, melt 1/2 tablespoon butter. Whisk 2 eggs with milk in a shallow bowl. Dip bread slices into egg mixture; cook in skillet until golden on both sides. Set aside; keep warm. Add remaining butter to skillet; break remaining eggs into skillet and cook over easy with yolks set. If desired, top eggs with cheese and cover. skillet until cheese melts. To assemble, place one slice bread on a plate; top with an egg, a sausage patty and a second slice of bread. Repeat to make a second sandwich. Slice in half and eat as a sandwich or drizzle with syrup and eat with a knife and fork. Makes 2 sandwiches.

Decorate clip clothespins by gluing on scraps of pretty scrapbooking paper. Add a button magnet on the back...oh-so handy for holding school photos, recipe cards and shopping lists on the refrigerator.

Toffee Apple French Toast

Patricia Wissler
Harrisburg, PA

This is so yummy and sweet! Make it the night before and pop it in the fridge...perfect for overnight weekend guests!

8 c. French bread, sliced into
   1-inch cubes and divided
2 Granny Smith apples, cored,
   peeled and chopped
8-oz. pkg. cream cheese,
   softened
3/4 c. brown sugar, packed

1/4 c. sugar
1-3/4 c. milk, divided
2 t. vanilla extract, divided
1/2 c. toffee or almond brickle
   baking bits
5 eggs, beaten

Place half the bread cubes in a greased 13"x9" baking pan; top with apples and set aside. In a medium bowl, beat cream cheese, sugars, 1/4 cup milk and one teaspoon vanilla until smooth. Stir in baking bits and spread over apples. Top with remaining bread cubes. In a separate bowl, beat eggs with remaining milk and vanilla; pour over bread. Cover and refrigerate for 8 hours to overnight. Remove from refrigerator 30 minutes before baking. Uncover and bake at 350 degrees for 35 to 45 minutes, until a knife inserted near the center comes out clean. Makes 8 servings.

An oilcloth tablecloth with brightly colored fruit and flowers is oh-so cheerful at breakfast...and sticky syrup and jam spills are easily wiped off with a damp sponge!

French Toast Berry Bake

Suzanne Vella
Babylon, NY

Our family loves to share this French toast bake for special family occasions like my son's birthday breakfast and when my sister's family visits from out of town. Both fresh and frozen berries are scrumptious, so you can enjoy this treat year 'round.

12 slices French bread, sliced
   1-inch thick
5 eggs, beaten
2-1/2 c. milk
1-3/4 c. brown sugar, packed
   and divided
1-1/2 t. vanilla extract
1-1/4 t. cinnamon

Optional: 1/2 t. nutmeg,
   1/4 t. ground cloves
Optional: 1 c. chopped pecans
1/2 c. butter, melted
2 c. blueberries, strawberries,
   raspberries and/or
   blackberries

Arrange bread slices in a greased 13"x9" baking pan; set aside. In a bowl, combine eggs, milk, one cup brown sugar, vanilla, cinnamon and desired spices. Whisk until blended; pour over bread. Cover and refrigerate for 8 hours to overnight. Let stand at room temperature 30 minutes before baking. Sprinkle with pecans, if using. Combine melted butter and remaining brown sugar; drizzle over top. Bake, uncovered, at 400 degrees for 30 minutes. Sprinkle with berries and bake an additional 10 minutes, or until a fork comes out clean. Serves 12.

Vintage-style salt shakers quickly become the prettiest little
containers for dusting powdered sugar or cinnamon
on breakfast treats.

Grandma Leona's Waffles

Beth Bundy
Long Prairie, MN

A very special recipe from a very special cook...my grandmother,
the best cook I've ever met.

4 eggs, separated
2 c. milk
1/4 c. butter-flavored
   shortening, melted and
   cooled

3 c. all-purpose flour
4 t. baking powder
1 t. salt
Garnish: sliced strawberries,
   whipped cream

In a large bowl, beat egg whites with an electric mixer on high setting until stiff peaks form. Add egg yolks, milk, shortening, flour, baking powder and salt; mix until smooth. Drop batter by 1/2 cupfuls into a greased waffle iron. Bake about 5 minutes, according to manufacturer's instructions. Serve topped with strawberries and whipped cream. Makes 8 servings.

Add a dash of whimsy to the breakfast table...serve up maple syrup in Grandma's vintage cow-shaped creamer.

Mom's Warm Spiced Milk

Janis Parr
Ontario, Canada

For many years now, I have made this soothing warm milk for my family. Once the chilly weather returns, a mug of this warms you up from the inside-out!

2 c. milk
2 t. vanilla extract
1/3 c. sugar

1/4 t. nutmeg
1/8 t. cinnamon

Combine milk, vanilla and sugar in a microwave-safe dish. Microwave on high setting for 3 to 3-1/2 minutes, until hot but not boiling. Stir in spices. Divide between 2 warmed mugs; serve hot. Serves 2.

Look for diner-style mugs at tag sales...made of thick white china, they really hold in the heat of a warm beverage. So cozy to wrap your hands around on a chilly morning!

Granny's Hot Cocoa

Faye O'Neal
Loganville, GA

*This was one of the first recipes my grandmother taught me when
I was just old enough to climb up on her kitchen step-stool to help.
A warm memory for those cold and snowy winter days!*

3/4 c. baking cocoa
1 c. sugar
1/4 c. water
4 c. milk
12-oz. can evaporated milk

1/2 t. cinnamon
1/8 t. salt
1 t. vanilla extract
Garnish: marshmallows or
  whipped cream

Combine cocoa, sugar and water in a saucepan. Mix well over
medium heat until smooth. Add milks, cinnamon and salt to cocoa
mixture. Heat over medium heat until hot and bubbly; do not boil.
Remove from heat; add vanilla extract. Mix well and ladle into mugs.
Add marshmallows or a dollop of whipped cream to each mug before
serving. Makes 6 servings.

Hot cocoa with warm cinnamon toast just like Grandma used to
make...yum! Toast slices of white bread and spread one side
generously with softened butter. Sprinkle with cinnamon-sugar
and broil for one to 2 minutes, until hot and bubbly.

GARDEN PATCH
Sides & Salads

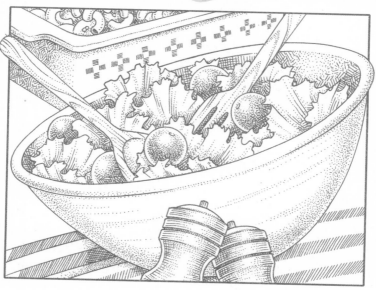

Crispy Potato Fingers

Lisa Johnson
Hallsville, TX

My mama always made these "tater fingers" for my kids when they would come for a visit. The kids are both grown now, and they still love it when Granny makes these yummy potatoes!

3 c. corn flake cereal
3 T. grated Parmesan cheese
1 t. paprika
1/4 t. garlic salt

1/4 c. butter, melted
2 baking potatoes, peeled and
cut into strips

Place cereal, cheese and seasonings into a blender or food processor. Process until crushed and well mixed. Pour cereal mixture into a pie plate or shallow dish; place melted butter in a separate shallow dish. Dip potato strips into butter, then into cereal mixture, coating well. Arrange potato strips on a greased baking sheet. Bake at 375 degrees for 25 minutes, or until tender and golden. Makes 4 servings.

"Sunday dinner at Grandma's" is a wonderful theme for a mini family reunion. Invite everyone to fix their favorite family recipes and bring them along. Whether it's a sit-down dinner or a simple picnic, you'll have a great time together!

Mom's Scalloped Potatoes

Susan Lacy
Bellingham, WA

These scalloped potatoes were a favorite when I was growing up...we still think they're scrumptious!

4 potatoes, peeled and thinly
   sliced
1 onion, sliced
6 slices Cheddar cheese
10-3/4 oz. can cream of
   mushroom soup

1 c. milk
1 t. salt
1/4 t. pepper
1/4 t. dried sage
Optional: 4 slices bacon

In a greased 2-1/2 quart casserole dish, layer 1/3 of the potato slices, 1/3 of the onion slices and 2 cheese slices. Combine soup, milk and seasonings; spoon 1/3 of soup mixture over potatoes. Repeat layers, ending with soup mixture. If desired, lay bacon slices over the top. Bake, uncovered, at 350 degrees for 1-1/4 hours, or until potatoes are tender. Serves 6.

Turn leftover mashed potatoes into tasty croquettes. Form into balls, dip into beaten egg and coat in dry bread crumbs, then fry in a little butter until golden on all sides.

Make-Ahead Potluck Potatoes

Tracy Ruiz
Las Vegas, NV

*My grandmother's tried & true recipe for church potlucks
and family get-togethers.*

12 russet potatoes, peeled,
  cubed and cooked
8-oz. pkg. cream cheese,
  softened
8-oz. container sour cream

1 t. onion powder
Optional: small amount milk
  or whipping cream
1/4 to 1/2 c. butter, melted
paprika to taste

Place warm potatoes in a large bowl; add cream cheese, sour cream
and onion powder. Mash until fluffy, adding a small amount of milk or
cream if desired. Spread in a greased 13"x9" baking pan. At this point,
the potatoes can be baked immediately or covered and refrigerated for
later. At baking time, drizzle with melted butter and sprinkle with a
little paprika. Bake, uncovered, for one hour, or until heated through
and golden. Makes 10 to 12 servings.

An ironstone pitcher filled
with old-fashioned lilacs will
bring to mind sweet memories
of Grandma's house. As the
seasons change, fill the pitcher
with fragrant peonies, herb
bundles and cheery sunflowers.

Hungarian Cabbage Noodles

Guyla Doughty
Allen Park, MI

My maternal grandmother brought this family favorite with her from Hungary. To make it her way, sprinkle it with a little sugar just before serving.

1/4 c. butter
1 head cabbage, shredded
2 T. salt
pepper to taste

16-oz. pkg. medium egg
 noodles or elbow macaroni,
 uncooked

Melt butter in a large saucepan over very low heat. Add cabbage, salt and pepper. Cover and cook for about 20 minutes, or until cabbage is tender. Meanwhile, cook noodles or macaroni according to package directions; drain. Add noodles or macaroni to cabbage and toss to mix. Makes 6 servings.

If becoming a grandmother was only a matter of choice,
I should advise every one of you straight away to become one.
There is no fun for old people like it.

-Hannah Whithall Smith

Jane's Broccoli Casserole

Jodi Griggs
Richmond, KY

Mom often made this for our Sunday dinner, and it was one of my absolute favorites as a little girl. Even today, when I go home to visit on Sundays I still enjoy this recipe of Mom's!

2 10-oz. pkgs. frozen broccoli
   flowerets, cooked and
   drained
2 T. butter
2 T. all-purpose flour
1 t. salt

2 c. milk
3-oz. pkg. cream cheese,
   softened
1 sleeve saltine crackers,
   crushed

Place cooked broccoli in a lightly greased 2-quart casserole dish and set aside. Melt butter in a saucepan over medium heat; stir in flour and salt. Gradually add milk; cook until mixture thickens, stirring frequently. Add cream cheese; stir until thoroughly blended. Pour sauce over broccoli. Cover well with cracker crumbs. Bake, uncovered, at 350 degrees about 15 to 20 minutes, until slightly golden and sauce is hot and bubbly. Serves 6.

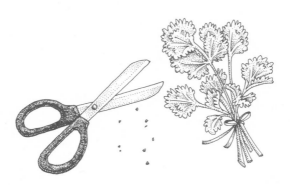

Kitchen shears are so handy for snipping fresh herbs,
cutting stewed tomatoes right in the can and snipping the ends
off fresh green beans. Just remember to wash them with
soap and water after each use.

Yellow Squash Bake

Tressie Salton
Charleston, WV

This recipe first became a favorite of mine when a relative brought it as a covered dish to our Sunday family dinner. My mom would fix it as soon as the squash was ready to pull from the vine. Even though we lived in the city, my dad always had a garden, no matter what!

2 lbs. yellow squash, peeled
    and diced
1 onion, chopped
10-3/4 oz. can cream of chicken
    soup
8-oz. container sour cream

1 c. carrots, peeled and
    shredded
8-oz. pkg. herb-flavored stuffing
    mix
1/2 c. margarine, melted

In a saucepan, cover squash and onion with water; bring to a boil over medium heat. Boil for 5 minutes; drain. In a large bowl, mix together soup and sour cream. Fold in carrots and squash mixture; set aside. Toss stuffing mix and melted margarine together. Spread half of stuffing mixture in a greased 12"x8" glass baking pan. Pour in squash mixture; top with remaining stuffing mixture. Bake, uncovered, at 350 degrees for 30 to 40 minutes. Cover with foil if needed to avoid overbrowning. Serves 6 to 8.

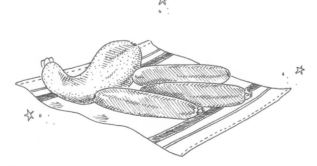

Zucchini and other summer squash make tasty side dishes
and are easily swapped out in recipes. Try substituting
old-fashioned yellow crookneck or pattypan squash
for zucchini in any favorite recipe.

Fancy Sunday Squash Dish

Virginia Shugart
Calhoun, GA

You'll love this creamy casserole with its golden crumb topping.

2 lbs. yellow squash, chopped
1/2 c. onion, chopped
1/2 c. water
8-oz. container sour cream
salt and pepper to taste
1/4 t. dried basil

1 c. soft bread crumbs
1/2 c. butter, melted
1/2 c. shredded Cheddar cheese
1/2 t. paprika
6 slices bacon, crisply cooked
    and crumbled

In a saucepan over medium heat, cook squash and onion in water until tender; drain and mash. Combine squash mixture, sour cream and seasonings. Pour into a greased 13"x9" baking pan. Toss together bread crumbs, butter, cheese and paprika; sprinkle over squash mixture. Top with bacon. Bake, uncovered, at 300 degrees for 20 minutes, or until hot and golden. Serves 6.

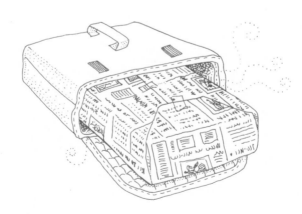

If you're taking a casserole to a potluck or carry-in dinner, keep it hot by covering the casserole dish with aluminum foil, then wrapping it in several layers of newspaper.

Great-Grandma's Green Beans

Heather Scukanec
Vancouver, WA

I am so glad to have this recipe from my great-grandmother, who lived to be ninety-nine years old. As soon as the aroma starts filling the air, I feel like I am five again, back at Great-Grandma's house.

6 slices bacon, chopped
1 c. onion, chopped
3 T. vinegar
2 T. all-purpose flour

16-oz. pkg. frozen French-cut
   green beans
salt to taste

In a skillet over medium heat, cook bacon until crisp; remove from skillet and set aside. Add onion to drippings; cook until golden. Add vinegar and flour; stir well. Add bacon and frozen green beans; completely cover skillet with lid. Reduce heat to low. Simmer for one hour, adding a little more water or vinegar as needed. Season with salt to taste. Serves 6 to 8.

Garden-fresh vegetables are delicious prepared simply...steamed and topped with pats of chive butter. To make, blend 1/4 cup softened butter with 2 tablespoons chopped fresh chives, one teaspoon lemon zest and a little salt & pepper.

Green Bean Baked Lucette

Bethany Zemaitis
Pittsburgh, PA

My husband's grandmother introduced me to this yummy green bean casserole. Now, it's often requested by my friends & family.

2 14-1/2 oz. cans green beans, drained and 1/4 c. liquid reserved
2 6-oz. cans French fried onions

3/4 c. shredded Cheddar cheese
10-3/4 oz. can cream of mushroom soup

In a lightly greased 2-quart casserole dish, alternate layers of green beans, onions and cheese. Mix soup and reserved liquid in a separate bowl; pour over bean mixture. Sprinkle remaining onions over casserole. Bake, uncovered, at 325 degrees for about 40 minutes. Serves 6 to 8.

An old pie safe makes a handy mini pantry for canned goods and boxed mixes. Dress it up with embroidered tea towels draped over the pierced-tin doors.

Gran's Mushrooms in Sour Cream

Shirl Parsons
Cape Carteret, NC

*This scrumptious recipe comes from my grandmother, Amelia Rudd,
my dad's mother who was from England.*

1 onion, chopped
2 T. butter
16-oz. pkg. sliced mushrooms
8-oz. container sour cream

1 t. dill weed
1/2 t. garlic powder
 salt and pepper to taste
Optional: 1 T. all-purpose flour

In a skillet over medium heat, sauté onion in butter until translucent. Add mushrooms; cook until lightly golden. Stir in sour cream and seasonings. If too thin, stir in flour. Cover and cook over low heat until heated through. Makes 4 to 6 servings.

Keep your wooden cutting board in tip-top shape. Protect it by coating lightly with olive oil and letting it stand for a few minutes. Pat dry with a paper towel; repeat several times. Set aside the board for 24 hours before using, then wash with hot, soapy water after each use.

Yoya's Spring Peas

Chris Lercel
Covina, CA

Yoya is our family nickname for Grandma, who has passed this recipe along to the grandkids. These very tender, tasty peas have become a favorite with us.

1 c. butter, sliced
1/2 head iceberg lettuce, very
   thinly sliced

2 10-oz. pkgs. frozen petite
   peas
1/2 to 1 t. sugar

Melt butter in a large saucepan over medium heat. Add lettuce and sauté until soft. Add frozen peas and sugar; stir. Reduce heat to low. Simmer for about one hour, stirring occasionally. Makes 8 servings.

It's so easy to make flavorful vegetable broth like Grandma's. Save up leftover veggies, scraps and peels in a freezer bag. Later, cover them with water and simmer gently for 30 minutes. Strain and freeze in ice cube trays...use to make delicious soups or add to any dish that needs a flavor boost!

Grandma Dumeney's Baked Beans

Susan Fountain
Stanton, MI

My Grandma Dumeney brought her sweet baked beans to every family reunion...everyone really looked forward to them! Grandma was eighty-four when she shared this simple recipe with me, and I'm so glad she did!

3 28-oz. cans pork & beans
1 lb. bacon, crisply cooked and
   crumbled

1 c. brown sugar, packed
1 c. catsup
1 onion, diced

Combine all ingredients in a large bowl and mix well. Transfer to a lightly greased 4-quart casserole dish with a lid. Bake, covered, at 400 degrees for one hour. Reduce temperature to 350 degrees; uncover dish and bake for an additional hour. Serves 8.

A fun idea for a family get-together! Serve up baked beans western style...enjoy them with a dinner 'round a campfire. Roast hot dogs, grill corn on the cob, roast potatoes in the coals and top dinner off with warm biscuits and honey. Bandanna napkins will keep everybody neat & tidy.

Granny's Cornbread Dressing

Kristin Freeman
Dundas, MN

My granny always made this whenever all my aunts, uncles, cousins and my family got together...luckily it feeds a crowd! The dressing may be prepared the day before and refrigerated, then baked at serving time.

4 8-1/2 oz. pkgs. cornbread
   mix
12-oz. pkg. chicken-flavored
   stuffing mix
4 slices bread, toasted and torn
1-1/2 c. onion, chopped
1-1/2 c. celery, chopped
1 c. plus 2 T. butter, diced and
   divided

10-3/4 oz. can cream of chicken
   soup
1/2 c. plus 2 T. milk
3 eggs, beaten
1 T. dried sage
3 to 4 14-1/2 oz. cans chicken
   broth

Bake cornbread mixes according to package directions. Cool; crumble and place in a large bowl. Add stuffing mix and bread; toss to mix and set aside. In a skillet over medium heat, cook onion and celery in 2 tablespoons butter until tender. Add onion mixture to cornbread mixture along with soup, milk, eggs and sage. Add broth to desired consistency. Divide between 2 greased 13"x9" baking pans; top with remaining butter. Bake, uncovered, at 350 degrees for about 45 minutes to one hour, until golden and heated through. Serves 12 to 16.

Counting calories? Make an easy substitution...try using evaporated milk instead of half-and-half, light cream soup instead of regular and thick Greek yogurt instead of sour cream. You'll get all the delicious richness, but with fewer calories.

Down-South Creamy Coleslaw

Staci Meyers
Montezuma, GA

*We all love this cool, refreshing coleslaw. It's great as a side
for your favorite BBQ ribs or pulled pork.*

3/4 c. mayonnaise
1 T. cider vinegar
1 T. sweet onion, grated and
   juice reserved
2 to 3 T. sugar
1/2 t. salt

1/4 t. pepper
1/4 t. celery seed
4 c. cabbage, shredded
1 c. carrots, peeled and
   shredded

In a large bowl, whisk together all ingredients except cabbage and
carrots. Add cabbage and carrots; toss to mix. Chill for at least 2 hours,
stirring once or twice while coleslaw chills. Stir well again at serving
time. Makes 6 to 8 servings.

A large clear glass bowl is a must-have for entertaining
family & friends. Serve up a layered salad, a pasta dish or
a sweet dessert trifle...even fill it with water and floating
candles to serve as a pretty centerpiece.

Louise's Potato Salad

Denise Neal
Castle Rock, CO

This recipe was handed down in my husband's family. His Portuguese grandma would make this often...it's one of the things they remember best about her cooking.

5 lbs. potatoes, peeled, cubed
    and cooked in salted water
4 eggs, hard-boiled, peeled and
    divided
1/4 c. mayonnaise
1/2 red onion, chopped

2 stalks celery, chopped
1 T. sweet pickle relish
1/2 t. celery salt
1/2 t. dried parsley
Garnish: paprika, fresh parsley

Keep potatoes warm while preparing other ingredients. Slice one egg and set aside for garnish. Dice remaining eggs; place in a large bowl and add remaining ingredients except garnish. Add potatoes to bowl while still warm; toss gently to coat. Garnish with sliced egg, paprika and parsley. Refrigerate until serving time. Makes 10 servings.

Next time you finish a jar of pickles, save the leftover pickle juice! It makes a tasty addition to potato salad and deviled eggs.

Granny's Macaroni Salad

Suzanne Morrow
Moorhead, MN

My family loves this cheesy macaroni salad made from my grandmother's own recipe. She was a very good granny to me!

48-oz. pkg. macaroni shells, uncooked
8-oz. pkg. pasteurized process cheese, cubed
1 green pepper, chopped
1 cucumber, shredded
4 to 5 carrots, peeled and shredded
2 tomatoes, chopped

Cook macaroni according to package directions. Drain and rinse with cold water. In a large serving bowl, mix cheese and vegetables together; add macaroni. Toss together. Add dressing and mix well. Chill 8 hours to overnight to allow flavors to combine. Serves 15 to 20.

Dressing:

2 c. mayonnaise-style salad dressing
2 T. sugar
2 T. vinegar
1 T. mustard

Mix together in a small bowl.

Spoon servings of pasta salad into hollowed-out tomato halves...so pretty on the dining table!

Aunt Nellie's Pasta Salad

Hope Davenport
Portland, TX

Aunt Nellie, who has long since passed away, was my grandma's aunt.
This recipe of hers has been in our family for quite awhile!

10-oz. pkg. rotini pasta,
    uncooked
4 eggs, hard-boiled, peeled and
    chopped
15-oz. can mixed vegetables,
    drained

1 pimento, chopped
1 c. sweet pickle relish
2 kosher gherkin pickles,
    chopped

Cook pasta according to package directions. Drain and rinse with cold water. In a large serving bowl, combine pasta, remaining ingredients and dressing. Stir until mixed well. Refrigerate until serving time. Serves 6 to 8.

Dressing:

2 c. mayonnaise
1/2 c. pasteurized process
    cheese, diced
1/2 c. sugar

1 T. onion, minced
1/2 t. celery salt
1/4 t. garlic powder

Mix together in a small bowl.

Make color copies of favorite snapshots from family picnics to découpage onto a picnic basket. Use paint pens to add family members' names and dates of best-remembered picnics...save some room for future memories!

Mama's Cucumber Salad

Virginia Shaw
Medon, TN

I used to take this salad to my sons' baseball award dinners and picnics. Children and adults alike always request this salad...it's cool, refreshing and very simple to make.

2 cucumbers, sliced
1 bunch green onions, diced,
   or 1 red onion, sliced and
   separated into rings

2 to 3 tomatoes, diced
16-oz. bottle zesty Italian salad
   dressing

Toss together vegetables in a large bowl; pour salad dressing over all and toss to mix. Cover and refrigerate at least 3 hours to overnight. Makes 8 to 10 servings.

Make an herb wreath...it's easy! Cover a grapevine wreath with sprigs of fresh herbs like sage, rosemary and thyme...simply slip long stems into the wreath until it's covered. Hung in a warm kitchen, the herbs will dry slowly and can be enjoyed year 'round.

Confetti Corn & Rice Salad

Lois Carswell
Kennesaw, GA

This colorful salad is a favorite at our family gatherings and barbecues, especially during the summer when we can use fresh-picked sweet corn...yum!

4 ears corn, husked
1-1/2 c. cooked rice
1 red onion, thinly sliced
1 green pepper, halved and
  thinly sliced
1 pt. cherry tomatoes, halved

Optional: 1 jalapeño pepper,
  thinly sliced
2 T. red wine vinegar
2 T. olive oil
salt and pepper to taste

Boil or grill ears of corn until tender; let cool. With a sharp knife, cut corn from cob in "planks." In a serving bowl, combine rice, red onion, green pepper, tomatoes and jalapeño pepper, if using. Top with corn planks and any remaining corn kernels. Drizzle with vinegar and oil; season with salt and pepper to taste. Serve at room temperature or refrigerate overnight before serving. Serves 8.

Toting a salad to a family get-together or a church potluck?
Mix it up in a plastic zipping bag instead of a bowl, seal and set it
on ice in a picnic cooler. No more worries about leaks or spills!

Crunchy Veggie Salad

Janie Branstetter
Duncan, OK

Mmm...with crunchy veggies, crisp bacon and creamy dressing, you're going to be asked for the recipe wherever you take this salad!

6 slices bacon, crisply cooked
    and crumbled
1 head cauliflower, cut into
    flowerets
1 bunch broccoli, cut into
    flowerets
1 c. radishes, sliced

3/4 c. green onion, diced
1 c. sour cream
1 c. favorite creamy salad
    dressing
.65-oz. pkg. cheese garlic salad
    dressing mix

In a large bowl, combine bacon and vegetables; set aside. In a separate bowl, mix together remaining ingredients. Pour salad dressing mixture over vegetables; toss to mix well. Chill 30 minutes before serving. Serves 6 to 8.

Country Buttermilk Dressing

Jocelyn Medina
Phoenixville, PA

Delicious drizzled on salad greens...makes a tasty dipping sauce too.

1 c. buttermilk
1 c. mayonnaise
1-1/2 T. onion powder
1-1/2 T. dried parsley

3/4 t. garlic powder
1/4 t. celery salt
1/4 t. salt
1/8 t. pepper

Mix all ingredients until smooth; transfer to a covered container. Keep refrigerated up to one week. Makes 2 cups.

Whip up some clever napkin rings in a jiffy! Sort through Grandma's button jar and string the prettiest ones on heavy elastic...delightful on rolled homespun napkins.

Easy Mandarin-Spinach Salad

Irene Robinson
Cincinnati, OH

*This fresh and fruity salad is scrumptious! Try it with sliced
strawberries and poppy seed dressing too.*

1-1/2 lbs. baby spinach
2 11-oz. cans mandarin
   oranges, drained

2-1/4 oz. pkg. sliced almonds,
   toasted
Italian salad dressing to taste

Combine spinach, oranges and almonds in a large salad bowl. Drizzle
with salad dressing. Makes 8 servings.

Grandma's Salad Oil

Phyllis Peters
Three Rivers, MI

An old-fashioned dressing for all kinds of greens and vegetables.

1 c. sugar
2 c. oil
1/2 c. white vinegar
2 t. salt

2 t. dry mustard
2 t. celery seed
1 t. onion, grated

Blend all ingredients well; pour into a covered container. May be kept
refrigerated for up to one month. Makes about 3-1/2 cups.

Estelle's Cornbread Salad

Hope Davenport
Portland, TX

This recipe came from my husband's grandma. I am so glad we have several of her recipes...they bring back memories of her with every delicious bite.

6-oz. pkg. cornbread mix
15-1/2 oz. can kidney beans,
    drained and rinsed
1 c. tomatoes, chopped
1 c. green peppers, chopped
2 bunches green onions,
    chopped

2 dill pickles, chopped
1 lb. bacon, crisply cooked and
    crumbled
1-1/2 c. mayonnaise
1/2 c. dill pickle juice

Bake cornbread mix according to package instructions. Cool; coarsely crumble into a large serving dish. Layer with beans, tomatoes, peppers, onions, pickles and bacon; set aside. Mix mayonnaise and pickle juice, blending well. Pour over layered salad and serve immediately. Serves 6.

Blanching makes fresh veggies crisp and bright...super for salads and dips. Bring a large pot of salted water to a rolling boil, add trimmed veggies and boil for 3 to 4 minutes, just until they begin to soften. Immediately remove veggies to a bowl of ice water. Cool, drain and pat dry.

Bountiful Garden Salad

Joanne Fajack
Youngstown, OH

Grandma always served this salad when we came to visit. We loved to watch her putting together this big beautiful bowl of pretty colors and wonderful tasting fruits. She grew most of the produce in her garden, and the nuts came from the grocery store where Grandpa helped out.

6 c. spinach, torn
1 lb. romaine lettuce, torn
1 stalk celery, chopped
1 red onion, chopped
1 tomato, chopped
1/2 cucumber, chopped
1 bunch fresh cilantro, chopped
1 clove garlic, finely chopped
1/2 orange, peeled and
   sectioned

3/4 c. blackberries, raspberries
   and/or blueberries
1/4 c. strawberries, hulled and
   sliced
1/4 c. chopped walnuts or
   pecans, toasted
Garnish: croutons

Place all of the ingredients except croutons into a large salad bowl and toss to mix. Drizzle with Raspberry Dressing; garnish with croutons. Serves 6 to 8.

Raspberry Dressing:

3/4 c. to 1 c. raspberries,
   crushed
1 c. oil
1/4 c. raspberry vinegar

1 T. sugar
2 T. lemon juice
salt and pepper to taste

Combine all ingredients except salt and pepper; whisk well. Add salt and pepper to taste.

Crisp Vegetable Salad Medley

Diane Chaney
Olathe, KS

A yummy, colorful make-ahead that feeds a crowd...just right for your next family reunion picnic.

2 c. green beans, cut into
    bite-size pieces
1-1/2 c. peas
1-1/2 c. corn
1 c. cauliflower, cut into
    bite-size pieces
1 c. celery, chopped
1 c. red onion, chopped

1 c. red pepper, chopped
15-oz. can garbanzo beans,
    drained and rinsed
4-oz. jar diced pimentos,
    drained
2 2-1/4 oz. cans sliced black
    olives, drained

In a large bowl, combine all ingredients. Add dressing and toss to coat. Cover and refrigerate for several hours to overnight, stirring occasionally. Serve with a slotted spoon. Makes 12 to 14 servings.

Dressing:

1 c. sugar
3/4 c. red wine vinegar
1/2 c. oil

1 t. salt
1/2 t. pepper

Whisk ingredients together in a small saucepan. Bring to a boil over medium heat; cool.

Shop the way Grandma did...at a nearby farmers' market! You'll find fresh fruits & vegetables, baked goods, jams & jellies...everything for a farm-fresh Sunday dinner.

Tomato-Mozzarella Salad

Joanna Nicoline-Haughey
Berwyn, PA

I remember Mom serving this simple salad in the summertime, made with fresh ingredients from Dad's wonderful garden full of sun-ripe red tomatoes, cucumbers, green peppers and herbs. What great memories!

4 tomatoes, cubed
1 cucumber, sliced
1 c. mozzarella cheese, cubed

1 T. fresh basil, chopped
1/4 c. extra virgin olive oil
salt and pepper to taste

Mix tomatoes, cucumber, cheese and basil together in a serving bowl. Drizzle with oil and toss to mix; sprinkle with salt and pepper. Serves 4.

Serve up a salad buffet for a warm-weather Sunday dinner!
Try a chicken or tuna salad, a potato or pasta salad, a crisp green tossed salad and a fruity gelatin salad. Crusty bread and a simple dessert complete a tasty, light meal.

Sweet-and-Sour Green Beans

Ellen Cooper
Mount Vernon, OH

This refreshing chilled side dish comes together in a jiffy, then waits in the fridge...so handy when you're putting together a big dinner!

1 lb. green beans, snapped into
   bite-size pieces
1 onion, sliced and separated
   into rings
3/4 c. sugar

1/4 c. oil
3/4 c. vinegar
1/2 t. celery seed
1/2 t. salt
1/4 t. pepper

Combine beans and onion in a serving bowl. Mix remaining ingredients and drizzle over bean mixture. Cover and chill for several hours before serving. Makes 6 to 8 servings.

Onion curls are a simple old-fashioned garnish. Cut the stem ends
of green onions lengthwise into lots of thin slices, place in
a bowl of ice water and soon the ends will begin to curl.

Copper Penny Carrots

Evelyn Love
Standish, ME

A tasty recipe that goes way back! It can be refrigerated for two to three weeks, so it's a handy make-ahead to keep on hand.

2 lbs. carrots, peeled and sliced
1 green pepper, thinly sliced
1 onion, chopped
10-3/4 oz. can tomato soup
1/2 c. oil

3/4 to 1 c. sugar
3/4 c. cider vinegar
1 t. Worcestershire sauce
1 t. mustard
salt and pepper to taste

In a saucepan over medium heat, cook carrots in salted water until almost tender; drain and rinse. Combine remaining ingredients in a separate saucepan. Bring to a boil over medium heat, stirring until thoroughly blended. Pour soup mixture over carrots. Cover and refrigerate until flavor is absorbed, at least 24 hours. Makes 10 to 12 servings.

Visit the farmers' market for the best homegrown veggies...toss a market basket in the car and let the kids pick out fresh flavors for Sunday dinner!

Grandmother's Red-Hot Salad

Tracee Cummins
Amarillo, TX

My great-grandmother was the perfect hostess. She always wore an apron and rarely sat down at family meals. Everything was always perfect at her table, from the sparkling china to the way the side dishes complemented the main course. She always served this salad at Easter alongside her beautiful baked ham...the spiciness of the salad is a perfect accompaniment to the mild flavor of ham.

1/2 to 1 c. red cinnamon candies
1 c. boiling water
3-oz. pkg. cherry gelatin mix
1 c. applesauce

Add desired amount of candies to boiling water, depending on how spicy you want your salad to be. Stir until candies are melted; strain out any unmelted bits. Stir in dry gelatin mix until dissolved; add applesauce and mix well. Pour into a serving dish; chill until set. Serves 6.

Grandmother could always be found wearing her apron...why not revive this useful tradition? Look through flea markets for some of the prettiest vintage aprons, or find a fun pattern and stitch one up in an afternoon.

Strawberry Ribbon Salad

Sandy Langford
Palmetto, GA

My great-grandmother and my great-aunt always served this salad at family reunions and church socials. From the time I was a little girl, I'd always look forward to "the red stuff" as I called it. Forty years later, it has become my own signature dish at get-togethers. I've inherited my grandmother's beautiful crystal bowl and still serve this sweet recipe in it. Each delicious spoonful reminds me of my relatives and of much simpler times.

1 c. boiling water
6-oz. pkg. strawberry gelatin
   mix
24-oz. container frozen sliced
   strawberries, thawed

1 c. chopped pecans
24-oz. container sour cream

In a large bowl, add boiling water to dry gelatin mix. Stir for at least 2 minutes, until gelatin is completely dissolved. Add thawed strawberries and juice; mix well. Stir in pecans. Chill in refrigerator until completely set. Once set, stir until combined. Spoon half of gelatin mixture into a serving bowl. Top with sour cream, smoothing evenly. Top with remaining gelatin mixture; chill for an additional hour before serving. Serves 10.

Toss sprigs or leaves of garden-fresh herbs like parsley, chives, mint, dill and basil into a lettuce salad for a delightfully different taste.

Heavenly Rice

Linda Robinson
Diamond, IL

My family enjoyed this yummy dish at every holiday for many years. Recently we were invited to my cousin's house for dinner, so I made Heavenly Rice and took it in the same bowl that my grandmother and mom had served it in. It brought back so many memories of family and togetherness!

3-oz. pkg. strawberry gelatin
   mix
1/2 c. powdered sugar
1 t. vanilla extract
1/2 c. boiling water

2 c. crushed pineapple, drained
1 c. cooked long-cooking rice,
   cooled
1 pt. whipping cream

Place dry gelatin mix, powdered sugar and vanilla in a large bowl; add boiling water and stir well. Add pineapple and rice; mix well. With an electric mixer on high setting, whip cream until stiff peaks form. Fold whipped cream into gelatin mixture. Spoon into a serving bowl; cover and refrigerate for 2 hours to overnight. Makes 10 servings.

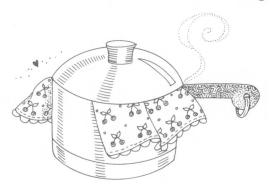

Steamed rice that's tender...never mushy! Cook long-cooking rice according to package directions. When it's done, remove pan from heat, cover with a folded tea towel and replace the lid. Let stand for 5 to 10 minutes, fluff with a fork and serve. The towel will absorb any excess moisture.

Apricot-Pineapple Jam

Carole Anne Barbaro
Clayton, NJ

This jam is simply delicious...it's one of my favorites! The recipe uses dried and canned fruit, so you can make it year 'round. Spoon it over vanilla ice cream for a real treat.

12-oz. pkg. dried apricots
1 c. water
20-oz. can crushed pineapple
1/2 c. orange juice

3 c. sugar
5 1/2-pint freezer containers
  and lids, sterilized

In a large saucepan over medium-high heat, bring apricots and water to a boil. Reduce heat; cover and simmer 15 minutes, or until apricots are tender, stirring occasionally. Mash apricots; add remaining ingredients. Simmer, uncovered, over low heat for one hour, or until thick and translucent, stirring frequently. Spoon jam into sterilized containers, leaving 1/2-inch headspace. Cool to room temperature, about one hour. Secure lids and let stand at room temperature until set, 8 to 24 hours. Jam is now ready to refrigerate up to 3 weeks or freeze up to one year. Makes 5 containers.

Keep pesky insects out of picnic pitchers of lemonade and iced tea. Simply clip four sparkly clip earrings to the corners of a table napkin and drape it over the open pitcher.

Candy Apple Jelly

Cyndy Rogers
Upton, MA

This scrumptious jelly's radiant glow makes it the perfect gift for anyone on your list, especially when decorated with an old-fashioned silver spoon and a doily under the ring. And so simple!

4 c. unsweetened apple juice
1/2 c. red cinnamon candies, crushed
1-3/4 oz. pkg. powdered pectin

4-1/2 c. sugar
6 1/2-pint canning jars and lids, sterilized

Combine apple juice, crushed candies and pectin in a large pot. Bring to a full boil over high heat, stirring constantly. Gently stir in sugar and return to a full boil. Boil 2 minutes. Remove from heat; skim foam if needed. Spoon into hot sterilized jars, leaving 1/4-inch headspace. Wipe rims; secure with lids and rings. Process in a boiling-water bath for 10 minutes. Set jars on a towel to cool. Check for seals. Makes 6 jars.

Choosing seeds for a kitchen garden? Look for heirloom varieties that Grandma & Grandpa may have grown. These fruits & veggies don't always look picture-perfect but their flavor can't be beat!

Lazy-Day Apple Butter

Pam Littel
Pleasant View, TN

This slow-cooker recipe is great when made on a rainy day. The house smells wonderful and it's the perfect afternoon snack.

5-1/2 lbs. cooking apples, cored, peeled and finely chopped
4 c. sugar
2 to 3 t. cinnamon
1/4 t. ground cloves
1/4 t. salt
4 1-pint freezer containers and lids, sterilized

Place apples in a slow cooker; set aside. Combine sugar, spices and salt; sprinkle over apples and mix well. Cover and cook on high setting for one hour. Reduce heat to low setting; cook for 7 to 10 hours, stirring occasionally, until thickened and dark brown. Uncover; continue to cook on low setting for one additional hour. Spoon apple butter into sterilized containers, leaving 1/2-inch headspace. Cool to room temperature, about one hour. Secure lids. Refrigerate apple butter up to 3 weeks or freeze up to one year. Makes 4 containers.

Homemade jams and preserves are always welcome gifts!
Wrap the jars with raffia, then glue an old-fashioned fabric
yo-yo on the bow. Top off the yo-yo with a pretty button.

Summer Berry Delight Jam

Bethi Hendrickson
Danville, PA

This jam will make you think of summer even on the coldest days of winter. Use 6 cups of any mix of berries you like.

3 c. strawberries, hulled
1 c. red raspberries
1 c. black raspberries
1 c. blueberries
1-3/4 oz. pkg. powdered pectin

1 t. lemon juice
1/2 t. butter
7 c. sugar
7 1/2-pint canning jars and
  lids, sterilized

Thoroughly crush berries in a blender. Place berries in a large saucepan and add pectin, lemon juice and butter. Bring to a boil over high heat; stir in sugar. Bring to a rolling boil for one minute, stirring constantly. Remove from heat; skim foam if needed. Spoon jam into hot sterilized jars, leaving 1/4-inch headspace. Wipe rims; secure with lids and rings. Process in a boiling-water bath for 20 minutes. Set jars on a towel to cool. Check for seals. Makes about 7 jars.

Vintage "day of the week" tea towels make the sweetest window valances...just drape them over the curtain rod.
So cheerful!

Apple-Ginger Chutney

Anna McMaster
Portland, OR

When we had Sunday dinner at my grandparents' house, Gran always had extra jars of this fruity, spicy relish for us to take home. It's delicious on roasted or grilled chicken...try it spooned over cream cheese on a cracker too. Yum!

4 Granny Smith apples, cored,
    peeled and chopped
2 c. onion, minced
1 red pepper, minced
1/4 c. fresh ginger, peeled and
    minced
1 c. golden raisins
1-1/2 c. cider vinegar

1-1/2 c. dark brown sugar,
    packed
3/4 t. dry mustard
3/4 t. salt
1/2 t. red pepper flakes
6 1/2-pint canning jars and
    lids, sterilized

Combine all ingredients in a large saucepan over medium-high heat. Bring to a boil, stirring frequently. Reduce heat to low. Simmer for 40 minutes, stirring occasionally, until thickened. Spoon chutney into sterilized jars; cool slightly and add lids. Keep refrigerated up to 2 weeks. Makes 6 jars.

Make a cut-glass relish tray sparkle like diamonds...it's easy! Wash it in mild dish soap, then rinse well with a mixture that's half plain warm water and half white vinegar. Pat dry with a lint-free towel...that's all it takes.

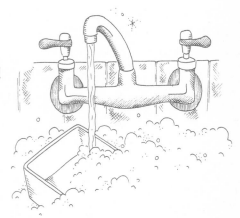

Nanny Boyd's Pickles

Kim Conner
South Boston, VA

For as long as I can remember, my grandmother, Inez Boyd, always had her homemade pickles on the table when we ate at her house. Five years ago when I decided to try making pickles myself, Nanny had passed away. Luckily my dad had all her recipes. I'll can one batch of cucumbers in slices and grind up another batch into pickle relish, ready to use in recipes...a spoonful really makes my homemade chicken salad delicious!

8 lbs. cucumbers, sliced
2 c. pickling lime
1-1/2 t. powdered alum
32-oz. bottle cider vinegar
32-oz. bottle white vinegar
5-lb. pkg. plus 1-1/2 c. sugar, divided
1-1/2 T. pickling spice
8 1-quart canning jars and lids, sterilized

Place cucumbers in a large enameled or stainless-steel pot; add enough water to cover. Add lime and alum; stir well. Cover and let stand overnight, stirring every so often. The next day, place cucumbers in a colander; drain and rinse very well. Rinse pot and return to stove; add vinegars and sugar to pot. Tie pickling spice in a square of muslin; add to pot along with cucumbers. Let stand for 2 hours. Bring to a boil over high heat; reduce heat to medium and simmer for 30 minutes. Discard spice bag. Pack pickle slices and liquid into hot sterilized jars, leaving 1/2-inch headspace. Wipe rims; secure with lids and rings. Process in a boiling-water bath for 10 minutes. Set jars on a towel to cool. Check for seals. Makes 8 jars.

For the crispest pickles, use fresh-picked cukes labeled as "pickling cucumbers" rather than regular salad cucumbers.

Crystal Pickle Chips

Vicki Holt
Valley View, TX

My grandma was a typical farm wife who cooked for my grandpa and their farmhands. She was such a fantastic cook and I inherited her recipe files when she passed on. I have always used zucchini and you'll be surprised how crisp they are! These are very similar to bread-and-butter pickles.

4 qts. zucchini or cucumbers, thinly sliced
5 onions, thinly sliced
2 green peppers, coarsely chopped
2 cloves garlic, chopped
1/2 c. pickling salt
4 qts. ice water

7 c. sugar
2 T. mustard seed
2 t. celery seed
2 t. turmeric
3 c. white vinegar
5 1-quart canning jars and lids, sterilized

Place vegetables in a large bowl; sprinkle with pickling salt. Add ice water and let stand at room temperature for 2 hours. Drain and set aside. Mix sugar and spices in a large enameled or stainless-steel pot; stir in vinegar. Bring just to a boil over high heat. Remove from heat. Pack vegetables into hot sterilized jars. Pour in hot liquid, leaving 1/2-inch headspace. Work out any bubbles by pressing down firmly with a spoon. Wipe rims; secure with lids and rings. Process in a boiling-water bath for 10 to 15 minutes. Set jars on a towel to cool. Check for seals. Makes 5 jars.

Fill a large Mason jar with vintage green-handled kitchen utensils to set on the kitchen counter...instant nostalgia!

Tangy Tomato Slices

Roberta Scheeler
Ashley, OH

When I was ten, I used to run to the woods and hide whenever I saw green tomatoes being picked...I didn't care if I never peeled another tomato! But now I enjoy making these tasty tomato slices...the tomatoes don't even need to be peeled.

12 green tomatoes, cored and
    sliced
1 T. salt
1 c. vinegar
1 c. water

1/2 c. sugar
6 to 8 1-pint canning jars and
    lids, sterilized
Optional: additional vinegar

In a large bowl, sprinkle tomatoes with salt. Let stand one hour at room temperature; drain. Transfer tomatoes to a large enameled or stainless-steel saucepan over medium-high heat; add remaining ingredients. Bring to a boil; boil for 5 minutes. Pack tomatoes in hot sterilized jars. Pour hot liquid over tomatoes, leaving 1/2-inch headspace. If there's not enough liquid, add one tablespoon vinegar and a little boiling water to to each jar. Wipe rims; secure with lids and rings. Process in a boiling-water bath for 20 minutes. Set jars on a towel to cool. Check for seals. Makes 6 to 8 jars, depending on size of tomatoes.

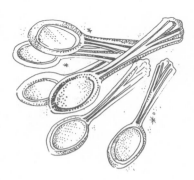

Silver-plated baby spoons are ideal for serving up dollops of mayonnaise, preserves, chutney and other condiments.

Best-Ever Garden Salsa

Annaley Wilkerson
Carmel, IN

Shortly after my husband and I were married, I was introduced to his grandmother's salsa...it was the best I've ever tasted! Ripe homegrown tomatoes were the secret. Grandma shared her recipe with me and I have been canning several batches every year for nearly twenty years. Lots of my friends use this recipe too. Grandma doesn't make salsa anymore, but her legacy lives on.

5 qts. tomatoes, peeled and
    quartered
3 green peppers, chopped
2 white onions, chopped
2 c. celery, diced
4 to 5 green Anaheim chiles,
    chopped
3 to 4 jalapeño peppers, seeded
    and chopped

3 to 4 yellow chiles, chopped
1/4 c. white vinegar
1/4 c. sugar
1/4 c. salt
1 T. pepper
1 T. paprika
1-1/2 t. ground cumin
10 to 12 1-pint canning jars
    and lids, sterilized

Combine all ingredients in a very large enameled or stainless-steel pot. Bring to a boil over high heat. Reduce heat to low; simmer for about one hour, stirring occasionally. Spoon vegetables and liquid into hot sterilized jars, leaving 1/2-inch headspace. Wipe rims; secure with lids and rings. Process in a boiling-water bath for 20 minutes. Set jars on a towel to cool. Check for seals. Makes 10 to 12 jars.

Better safe than sorry! Always wear plastic gloves to protect your hands when chopping hot peppers.

Sweet-and-Sour Kraut Relish

Lena Butler Smith
Pickerington, OH

This simple recipe started with my great-grandmother, Clara Belle Butler. Over the years, I have changed it up a bit to meet changing tastes. This homemade relish tastes great on hamburgers, hot dogs and steaks...try it at your next family cookout!

2 c. sugar
1 t. celery seed
1 t. salt
2-1/2 c. sauerkraut, drained
    and rinsed

1/4 c. red pepper, chopped
1/4 c. yellow pepper, chopped
1/2 c. pimentos, chopped
1/2 c. red onion, chopped

In an enameled or stainless-steel saucepan, mix sugar, celery seed and salt; bring to a boil over high heat, then reduce to medium-high. Mixture makes its own liquid. Boil for 2 minutes and remove from heat. Cool. Add remaining ingredients and mix well. Ladle into a covered container. Refrigerate for at least 2 hours before serving; keep refrigerated. Makes 18 to 24 servings.

Hosting a Sunday cookout for family & friends? Serve nostalgic soft drinks like root beer, orange pop and grape fizz in glass bottles, just for fun!

End-of-the-Garden Relish

Cheri Maxwell
Gulf Breeze, FL

When I was growing up, I always got to spend the last couple weeks of my summer vacation at my grandparents' home in the country. Grandma was justifiably proud of her big backyard garden. She would send me out with a basket to find the last of the vegetables growing there, so she could make this relish that we all loved. Just a taste of it still brings back such memories!

8 c. green tomatoes, cored and chopped
4 c. red tomatoes, cored, peeled and chopped
4 c. cabbage, chopped
3 c. onions, chopped
2 c. celery, chopped
1 c. green peppers, chopped
1 c. red peppers, chopped
1 c. cucumbers, chopped
1/2 c. canning salt
2 32-oz. bottles white vinegar
4 c. brown sugar, packed
2 cloves garlic, minced
1 T. celery seed
1 T. mustard seed
1 T. cinnamon
1 t. ground ginger
1/2 t. ground cloves
8 1-pint canning jars and lids, sterilized

In a very large enameled stockpot, combine chopped vegetables and salt; toss to thoroughly. Cover and refrigerate for 12 to 18 hours. Transfer vegetables to a colander; drain thoroughly. In the same stockpot, combine remaining ingredients. Simmer over medium-high heat for 10 minutes, stirring occasionally. Add vegetables; reduce heat and simmer, uncovered, for 30 minutes, stirring occasionally. Increase heat; bring to a boil. Spoon vegetables and liquid into hot sterilized jars, leaving 1/2-inch headspace. Wipe rims; secure with lids and rings. Process in a boiling-water bath for 15 minutes. Set jars on a towel to cool. Check for seals. Makes 8 jars.

TUMMY-WARMING
Soups & Breads

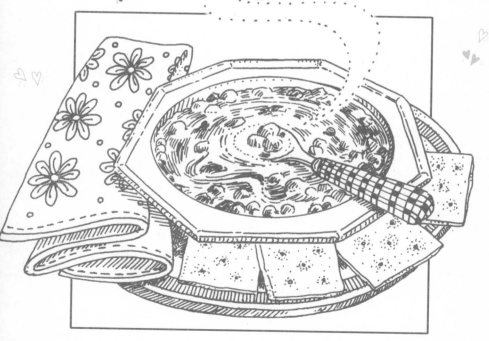

Gram's Creamy Chicken Noodle Soup

Sandy Coffey
Cincinnati, OH

*This is my one-of-a-kind chicken noodle soup. It goes well with
peanut butter & jelly sandwiches any time of year...real comfort food!*

2 lbs. boneless, skinless chicken
  breasts, diced
10 c. water
2 T. chicken bouillon granules
4 t. dried parsley
2 t. dried thyme
1/2 t. pepper
2 bay leaves

4 c. carrots, peeled and sliced
2 c. celery, diced
2 c. onion, chopped
8-oz. pkg. medium egg noodles,
  uncooked
4 c. milk, divided
1/2 c. all-purpose flour

In a large soup pot, combine chicken, water, bouillon and seasonings.
Bring to a boil over medium-high heat. Add vegetables and noodles;
return to a boil. Reduce heat to medium; cover and simmer 20 to
30 minutes, until vegetables are tender. Meanwhile, in a small
covered container, combine one cup milk and flour; shake well until
smooth. Stir into soup along with remaining milk. Continue cooking
over medium heat until thickened and heated through. Discard bay
leaves before serving. Makes 16 servings.

Soup is so nice when shared. Thank a friend with a basket of
warm rolls and a pot of steaming homemade soup.
What a welcome surprise on a brisk day!

Homemade Soup Noodles

Patricia Tiede
Cheektowaga, NY

My mom always made these tender noodles for her chicken soup. She also served them tossed with butter as a hearty side dish. These can be made very quickly in your stand mixer with the dough hook. They're well worth the effort!

1-1/2 c. all-purpose flour
3/4 t. salt

3 large or 4 small eggs, beaten

Combine all ingredients in a bowl; mix with a fork until dough forms. If too dry, add a few drops of water. Knead dough several times on a floured surface; roll out until very thin. Cut dough into thin strips or squares, as desired. Lay noodles on floured surface. Bring a large saucepan of water to a boil over high heat. Add noodles; boil about 15 minutes, until noodles rise to the top and puff up. Drain; add to hot soup or toss with butter. Makes about 6 servings.

Keep a stash of aprons in big and little sizes for everyone who wants to help out in the kitchen!

Country Corn & Cheddar Chowder

Vicki Callahan
Saint Peters, MO

With sweet corn and other fresh-picked vegetables, this made-from-scratch soup is just delicious! When corn isn't in season, substitute 3 cups frozen corn kernels.

6 ears corn, husked
3 T. butter, melted and divided
1 c. onion, diced
2 stalks celery, diced
1 leek, split and diced
1 red pepper, diced
2 t. ground cumin

1 t. ground coriander
1/2 t. cayenne pepper
1/2 t. salt
8 c. chicken broth
8-oz. pkg. shredded extra sharp
   Cheddar cheese

Brush the ears of corn lightly with one tablespoon melted butter. Grill or broil corn until roasted on all sides, about 5 minutes. Slice off kernels, reserving the cobs. Add remaining butter to a large, heavy soup pot over medium heat. Add corn, remaining vegetables and seasonings; sauté until vegetables are soft but not browned. Pour in broth. Bring to a boil; reduce to a simmer and add reserved corn cobs. Simmer 40 to 45 minutes, stirring occasionally. Discard cobs; stir in cheese and serve immediately. Serves 8.

When cutting the kernels from ears of sweet corn, here's a clever way to keep them from flying all over the kitchen. Simply stand the ear in the center tube of an angel food cake pan...the kernels will fall neatly into the pan.

Cream of Broccoli Soup

Sara Tatham
Plymouth, NH

This is our family's favorite broccoli soup. The bay leaves in this recipe make all the difference to the flavor! It doesn't call for cheese like most broccoli soup recipes, so it's a little bit healthier too.

3 c. chicken broth
1 bunch broccoli, chopped
1 onion, chopped
3 bay leaves

6 T. butter, sliced
1/4 c. plus 3 T. all-purpose flour
3 c. milk
salt and pepper to taste

In a Dutch oven over medium heat, bring broth to a boil. Add broccoli, onion and bay leaves. Reduce heat; cover and simmer until broccoli is tender. Discard bay leaves. In a separate saucepan, melt butter over medium heat. Stir in flour until smooth and bubbly. Remove from heat; gradually stir in milk. Return pan to heat and cook over medium heat, stirring often, until mixture is hot and thickened. Add one cup broccoli mixture to milk mixture, stirring until well blended. Gradually add all of milk mixture to broccoli mixture in the Dutch oven. Stir to combine well; cook and stir until well blended. Add salt and pepper to taste. Serves 4 to 6.

Yellowware soup bowls make any soup supper extra special.
Pick up a set of vintage-style new bowls or collect old ones
at antique shops...mix & match for fresh farmhouse style.

Grandma Jo's Potato Soup

Hope Davenport
Portland, TX

*My grandma has been making this satisfying soup for as long as
I can remember. We really enjoy it on a chilly afternoon.*

2 lbs. potatoes, peeled and diced
1/2 lb. carrots, peeled and diced
2 stalks celery, diced
1 onion, diced
4 c. water
12-oz. can evaporated milk
1/4 c. butter, sliced

onion and garlic seasoned salt
   to taste
pepper to taste
8-oz. pkg. shredded Cheddar
   cheese
3 slices bacon, crisply cooked
   and crumbled

Combine vegetables and water in a stockpot over medium-high heat.
Cook until vegetables are fork-tender, 15 to 20 minutes. Reduce heat
to low; stir in evaporated milk, butter and seasonings. Heat through.
Ladle into soup bowls; garnish with cheese and bacon. Serves 6.

Evaporated milk was an old standby in Grandma's day...it's still
oh-so handy because it's extra creamy and needs no refrigeration.
Keep several cans in the pantry to use in soups and gravies
that call for regular milk.

Sunday Meeting Tomato Soup

Gretchen Ham
Pine City, NY

Fresh basil really makes this soup special. It's often requested at our church's Sunday soup & sandwich lunches after church services.

1/2 c. butter, sliced
1 c. fresh basil, chopped
2 28-oz. cans crushed tomatoes
2 cloves garlic, minced

2 pts. half-and-half
salt and pepper to taste
Garnish: croutons, grated
    Parmesan cheese

In a large saucepan, melt butter over medium heat. Add basil; sauté for 2 minutes. Add tomatoes and garlic; reduce heat and simmer for 20 minutes. Remove from heat; let cool slightly. Working in batches, transfer tomato mixture to a blender and purée. Strain into a separate saucepan and add half-and-half, mixing very well. Reheat soup over medium-low heat; add salt and pepper to taste. Serve topped with croutons and grated Parmesan cheese. Makes 10 servings.

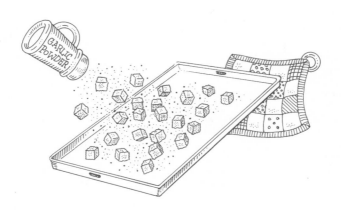

Savory homemade croutons are easy to make. Toss cubes of day-old bread with olive oil, garlic powder, salt and pepper. Place bread cubes in a single layer on a baking sheet and bake at 400 degrees for about 10 minutes, or until toasty.

Mom's Chicken-Veggie Soup

Marilyn Petersen
Boulder City, NV

Mmm...nothing says "I love you" like a bowlful of chicken soup
brimming with noodles and vegetables.

1 to 2 T. olive oil
1/2 c. onion, chopped
2 T. garlic, chopped
1 c. carrots, peeled and diced
1 potato, peeled and diced
1 c. celery, diced
6 to 8 c. chicken broth
15-oz. can tomato sauce

1 c. boneless, skinless chicken,
  diced
3/4 c. frozen corn
1/2 c. frozen peas
2 t. dried parsley
1 t. lemon-pepper seasoning
1-1/2 c. wide egg noodles,
  uncooked

Heat oil in a large soup kettle over medium heat. Add onion and garlic; sauté for 3 to 5 minutes, until onion is translucent. Stir in carrots, potato and celery; sauté for an additional 8 to 10 minutes. Add remaining ingredients except noodles; simmer for 10 to 12 minutes. Add noodles and cook until tender, about 10 minutes. Makes 8 servings.

Need to add a little zing to a soup or stew? Just add a dash of herb-flavored vinegar...a super use for that bottle you brought home from the farmers' market.

Grandma's Pastina

Michelle McFadden-DiNicola
Highland Park, NJ

This is an old family recipe that my grandma used to make for us when we weren't feeling well. It's deceptively simple...and really delicious and cozy!

4 c. water
3 cubes chicken bouillon
2 cubes beef bouillon
3/4 c. tiny star or alphabet
   soup pasta, uncooked

1/2 c. fresh parsley, coarsely
   chopped
1/8 t. pepper
2 eggs
salt and pepper to taste

Place water and bouillon cubes in a soup pot over medium heat. Stir to break up bouillon cubes once the water is simmering. Stir in pasta, parsley and pepper; boil until pasta is tender, 3 to 4 minutes. Turn heat down to lowest possible setting. In a small bowl, whisk eggs lightly with a fork; season with salt and pepper. While stirring the soup slowly, pour in eggs. Continue stirring until eggs begin to turn white. Allow eggs to cook thoroughly, about one additional minute. Serve hot. Makes 2 to 3 servings.

Make a family recipe book of all the best handed-down family favorites. Tie it all up with a bow and slip a family photo in the front...a gift to be treasured.

Gramble's Vegetable Soup

Sandy Coffey
Cincinnati, OH

This was my mom's famous soup and now it's mine. Since my grandkids are not fond of canned soup, they named mine "Gramble's" vegetable soup. This soup simmers for several hours, and it's well worth the wait. Yum...good to the last spoonful!

1 lb. stew beef, diced
1 onion, chopped
5 stalks celery, chopped
1 head cabbage, chopped
28-oz. can whole tomatoes
29-oz. can tomato purée
16-oz. pkg. frozen mixed
   vegetables

14-oz. can corn, drained
14-oz. can peas, drained
14-oz. can green beans, drained
14-oz. can sliced carrots,
   drained
salt and pepper to taste

In a large stockpot over medium heat, place beef, onion, celery and cabbage; add enough water to cover. Reduce heat to low; cover and simmer for one hour, stirring occasionally. Add undrained tomatoes and tomato purée; continue simmering for 30 minutes. Stir in frozen vegetables and simmer another hour. Mix in remaining ingredients and simmer another hour. Makes about 15 servings.

Be sure to bring out all the old family photo albums at your next family gathering. They're sure to spark fun conversation as guests look at pictures they haven't seen in years!

Nonnie's Italian Wedding Soup

Liz Roaden
Miamisburg, OH

This recipe was in our family long before I came along! My grandmother always served it at holiday dinners. We still have it on special days...when she passed on, my mom and then my youngest sister took over making the wedding soup. It brings back such memories!

18 c. water
4 boneless, skinless chicken
   breasts
1 yellow onion, peeled
1 c. celery, diced
1 c. carrot, peeled and diced
12 to 15 cubes chicken bouillon,
   or to taste

2 10-oz. pkgs. frozen chopped
   spinach, thawed
Optional: frozen mini meatballs,
   uncooked acini de pepe or
   orzo pasta
Garnish: croutons

In a 6-quart stockpot, combine water, chicken and whole onion. Bring to a boil over medium-high heat. Reduce heat to medium and cook until chicken juices run clear, 10 to 15 minutes. Remove onion and discard. Remove chicken and shred; return to pot. Add celery and carrot; continue to simmer, uncovered, for 45 minutes. Stir in bouillon, spinach and meatballs, if using; simmer over low heat an additional 30 minutes. If desired, stir in pasta about 5 minutes before soup is done. Garnish with croutons. Makes about 25 servings.

When you look at your life, the greatest happinesses
are family happinesses.

-Dr. Joyce Brothers

Mini Ham & Cheesewiches

Elisa Thompson
Celina, TN

*I always take these little sandwiches to family gatherings.
I have a very large family, so I have to fix lots!*

17-oz. pkg. brown & serve
   dinner rolls
8-oz. pkg. sliced deli ham

12 slices American cheese
Garnish: melted butter,
   garlic salt

Slice each roll in half like a hamburger bun. Place a slice of ham and a
slice of cheese on each roll bottom. Add tops; brush with butter and
sprinkle with garlic salt. Arrange on an ungreased baking sheet. Bake
at 450 degrees until golden and cheese is melted. Makes one dozen.

A sweet way to remember Sunday dinner at Grandma's
house...use a vintage flowered hankie as a mat
for her handwritten recipe cards.

Granny's Tin Can Soup

Barb Pitcock
Bowling Green, KY

My granny had a large family and this soup, served with fresh bread, filled a lot of hungry tummies. I would like to dedicate this recipe to my sister, Norma, whom I love dearly. The two of us played with this recipe until we perfected it. I hope you enjoy it as much as we do!

1 lb. ground beef, browned and
  drained
15-oz. can diced tomatoes
15-oz. can diced tomatoes with
  chiles
15-1/2 oz. can chili beans
15-oz. can corn

2 10-3/4 oz. cans vegetarian
  vegetable soup
10-3/4 oz. can tomato soup
16-oz. can sliced potatoes,
  drained
14-1/2 oz. can sliced carrots,
  drained

Combine all ingredients in a large stockpot. Bring to a simmer over medium heat. Reduce heat and simmer, uncovered, for 35 to 40 minutes, stirring occasionally. Makes 8 to 10 servings.

Grandma's stove always had a pot of savory soup bubbling on a back burner...use a slow cooker to cook up the same slow-simmered flavor! A favorite soup recipe that simmers for one to 2 hours on the stove can cook for 6 to 8 hours on the low setting without overcooking.

Grandma Logsdon's Beef Stew

Teresa Amert
Upper Sandusky, OH

My mother may have gotten this recipe from her mother-in-law, since Mama "didn't know how to boil water" as a 19-year-old bride. Mama used our own beef, and of course, all the vegetables came from our garden. We kids did the hoeing and weeding and shelled the peas and beans. Since there were so many of us, it didn't take that long! This stew is delicious with baking powder biscuits, hot from the oven.

1-1/2 lbs. beef round steak, cut
    into bite-size pieces
1 T. oil
1/4 c. all-purpose flour
2-1/2 c. water, divided
1 c. tomato juice or sauce
5 potatoes, peeled and quartered

1 onion, sliced
2 carrots, peeled and chopped
1 stalk celery, chopped
1/2 c. peas
Optional: 1/2 c. green beans
salt and pepper to taste

In a large soup pot over medium heat, brown beef in oil. Drain; sprinkle with flour and mix in. Slowly add 1/4 cup water; stir well. Add tomato juice or sauce and an additional 1/4 cup water; stir together and bring to a boil. Stir in remaining water; add remaining ingredients. Cook, partially covered, over low heat until beef and vegetables are tender, about one hour. Ladle into rimmed dinner plates. Serves 4.

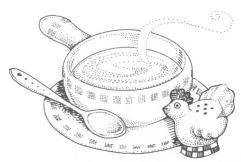

Plan ahead for soups and stews that are practically fat-free.
Simmer soup the day before, refrigerate overnight and
simply lift off the fat that solidified on the top.

Plenty o' Veggies Beef Stew

*Paula Marchesi
Lenhartsville, PA*

Years ago, when I helped my mom in the kitchen, there was no such thing as a slow cooker. Well, times have changed. This is a version of my mom's recipe which for years has been a mainstay in our home. Perfect for today's slow cooker!

8 slices bacon, diced
3 lbs. stew beef, cubed
6 carrots, peeled and thickly
   sliced
6 tomatoes, peeled and cut into
   wedges
4 potatoes, peeled and cubed
3 c. butternut squash, peeled
   and cubed

1/2 c. frozen lima beans
1/2 c. corn
2 cloves garlic, minced
2 t. dried thyme
2 14-1/2 oz. cans beef broth
6 c. cabbage, chopped
1/2 t. celery salt
1/2 t. pepper

In a large skillet over medium heat, cook bacon until crisp. Remove bacon to paper towels with a slotted spoon and refrigerate; reserve pan drippings. Brown beef in batches in reserved drippings; drain. In a 6-quart slow cooker, combine carrots, tomatoes, potatoes, squash, beans, corn, garlic and thyme. Top with beef. Pour broth into slow cooker. Cover and cook on low setting for 8 hours. Stir in cabbage and seasonings. Cover; increase to high setting and cook for 30 to 35 minutes, until cabbage is tender. Sprinkle servings with bacon. Makes 10 to 12 servings.

Pass along Grandma's soup tureen or kettle to a new bride...fill it with jars of favorite seasonings and tie on a cherished soup recipe.

Aunt Jessie's Welch Stew

Ida Mannion
North Chelmsford, MA

This simple recipe is from my husband's grandmother. He still remembers how the aroma of this stew would make him feel comfy and warm.

4 slices bacon, diced
1 onion, finely chopped
1 green pepper, chopped
1-1/2 lbs. ground beef

2 10-3/4 oz. cans tomato soup
2 15-oz. cans pork & beans
salt and pepper to taste

In a large saucepan over medium heat, cook bacon until crisp. Add onion and pepper; sauté until translucent. Add ground beef and brown; drain. Stir in remaining ingredients; simmer over low heat for 15 to 20 minutes. Makes 2 to 4 servings.

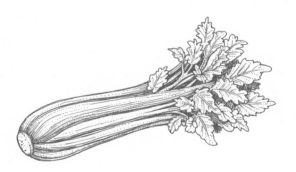

Add flavor to soups with dried celery leaves. Spread fresh celery leaves on a baking sheet and bake at 180 degrees for about 3 hours. When they're crisp, store them in a canning jar. To use, crumble the leaves into the soup pot.

Grandma Hallie's Spicy Chili

Ashley Hull
Virden, IL

This recipe is from my Great-Grandma Hallie. I am so glad I actually have one of her recipes written down! She would make the best food and say, "Honey, it's all up here," meaning she memorized all her recipes. This recipe shows what a wonderful cook she was!

2 lbs. ground beef
1/4 c. dried, minced onion
2 t. salt
2 10-3/4 oz. cans tomato soup
2 16-oz. cans kidney beans

2-1/2 c. water
1 t. Worcestershire sauce
2 T. butter, sliced
3 T. chili powder

In a large soup pot, brown beef over medium heat; drain. Add remaining ingredients; reduce heat to medium-low. Simmer for 45 minutes, stirring occasionally. Makes 8 to 10 servings.

Pour herbs and spices into your hand before adding them to a kettle of hot soup. Sprinkling herbs right from the container over hot food can cause them to absorb steam and clump.

Abigail's Crusty White Bread

Abigail Smith
Gooseberry Patch

My mother used to bake a version of this bread in early summer. We enjoyed it hot from the oven with fresh butter and strawberry jam, homemade with berries from her patch...a tradition I now share with my own children.

2-1/2 c. water
1 T. active dry yeast
1 T. sugar
1 T. salt

7 c. all-purpose flour, divided
1/4 to 1/2 c. butter, softened
    and divided

Heat water until very warm, about 110 to 115 degrees. In a large bowl, combine 1/2 cup warm water, yeast and sugar. Stir until foamy; let stand for 5 minutes. Add remaining water, salt and 3-1/2 cups flour. Blend with an electric mixer on low speed, using a dough hook if available. Add remaining flour, 1/4 cup at a time. Beat on medium speed for 10 minutes, until dough is smooth and elastic. Beat in butter, one tablespoon at a time. Place dough in a lightly greased bowl, turning to coat. Cover with a tea towel; set in a warm place. Let rise for 45 minutes, until double in bulk. Punch down dough and turn out onto a floured surface; divide in half. Roll out each half into a 12-inch by 9-inch rectangle. Fold each rectangle into thirds, pinching seam closed. Place loaves in 2 greased 9"x5" loaf pans, seam-side down. Cover again and let rise until double, about 45 minutes. Bake at 375 degrees for 35 to 45 minutes, until golden. Cool on a wire rack. Makes 2 loaves.

Keep fresh-baked rolls hot alongside servings of soup. Before arranging rolls in a bread basket, place a terra-cotta warming tile in the bottom and line with a flowered tea towel.

Jai Lai Herb Butter

Karen McCann
Marion, OH

A central Ohio restaurant used to be famous for serving this fantastic butter with their rolls. My family loves it! I'm sure yours will too.

1 lb. butter
4 t. lemon juice
1/2 t. garlic powder
1 t. dried oregano

1 t. dried chives
1 t. dried thyme
1 t. dried rosemary
1 t. dried tarragon

Place butter in a bowl; soften to room temperature. Add lemon juice and garlic powder; blend until smooth. Finely crush herbs and add to butter mixture; mix well. Spoon into a covered crock or form into logs and wrap in plastic wrap. Chill overnight before serving. May be frozen; allow to thaw in refrigerator. Makes one pound.

Cooked Cheese

Judy Scherer
Benton, MO

My great-grandmother used to make this yummy spread. It's been a family tradition ever since.

16-oz. container cream-style
   cottage cheese
1-1/2 t. baking soda

1/2 c. margarine, sliced
3/4 c. pasteurized process
   cheese spread, diced

Spoon cottage cheese into a bowl. Sprinkle with baking soda; let stand 2 hours. Place margarine and cheese spread in a heavy saucepan over low heat. Stir until melted; mix together and add cottage cheese mixture. Cook and stir over low heat until thin and smooth. Serve warm as a spread for bread. Makes 8 servings.

Swope Bread

Dan Needham
Columbus, OH

My grandmother used to make this simple batter bread. We never did find out where the name came from, but it is tasty and easy to make.

2 c. whole-wheat flour
1 c. all-purpose flour
1/2 c. sugar

1 t. salt
2 t. baking soda
2 c. buttermilk

In a large bowl, stir together flours, sugar and salt; set aside. In a separate bowl, dissolve baking soda in buttermilk. Stir buttermilk mixture into flour mixture; beat well. Pour batter into a lightly greased 9"x5" loaf pan. Bake at 350 degrees for one hour, until golden. Cool on a wire rack. Makes one loaf.

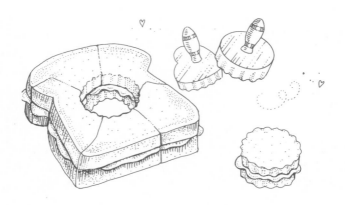

Turn slices of bread into jigsaw puzzles...dinnertime fun for the kids! Butter bread slices and use a cookie cutter to slice a shape through the center. Then cut the surrounding bread into puzzle pieces with a kitchen knife. Mix up the pieces before serving the sandwich.

Cloverleaf Oat Rolls

Sharon Crider
Junction City, KS

It wouldn't be Sunday dinner at Grandma's without a basket of her delicious homemade rolls on the dinner table!

1 c. quick-cooking oats, uncooked
1/3 c. brown sugar, packed
1 t. salt
1/3 c. shortening

1-1/2 c. boiling water, divided
1 env. active dry yeast
4 c. all-purpose flour, divided
1 egg, beaten

Place oats, brown sugar, salt and shortening in a large bowl; pour 1-1/4 cups boiling water over all. Let stand until lukewarm. In a separate small bowl, let remaining water cool slightly; sprinkle with yeast and stir until dissolved. Add yeast mixture to oat mixture along with 2 cups flour and egg. Beat until well blended. Add remaining flour, a little at a time, to make a soft dough. Turn onto a lightly floured surface; knead until smooth and elastic. Place dough in a greased bowl; turn so top is greased. Cover with a tea towel; let rise in a warm place until double in bulk, about 1-1/2 hours. Punch down; let rise again until double, about 30 minutes. Form into one-inch balls; place 3 balls in each cup of greased muffin tins. Let rise again until double, 20 to 30 minutes. Bake at 375 degrees for about 25 minutes, until golden. Makes about 2-1/2 dozen.

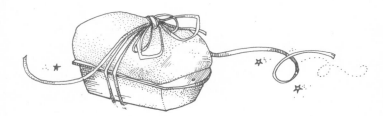

When baking bread, if the water added to yeast is too hot, it will kill the yeast. Use Grandma's old trick to test the temperature...sprinkle the heated water on your forearm. If it doesn't feel either hot or cold, the temperature is just right.

Homemade Butter Rolls

Deborah Goodrich
Smithfield, VA

These scrumptious rolls are a must for our family's holiday dinners.
We smoke our own ham, so they go hand-in-hand around here on
our farm. Try them split and filled with thin slices of ham...yum!

1 c. water
1 env. active dry yeast
1/2 c. sugar, divided
3 eggs, beaten

3/4 t. salt
4-1/2 c. all-purpose flour
1/2 c. butter, melted

Heat water until very warm, about 110 to 115 degrees. In a large
bowl, sprinkle warm water with yeast and 2 tablespoons sugar. Stir;
let stand 5 minutes. Stir in remaining sugar, eggs and salt. Gradually
stir in enough flour to make a soft dough. Cover and let rise for about
1-1/2 hours, or until double in bulk. Punch down. Use the melted
butter to coat hands generously; form dough into 2 dozen rolls. Place
rolls into 2 greased 13"x9" baking pans. Cover and let rise again until
double, about 2 hours. Bake at 400 degrees for 10 minutes, or until
golden. Makes 2 dozen.

Give breads and rolls a beautiful finish. Whisk together
a tablespoon of water with an egg yolk for a golden finish,
or an egg white for a shiny luster. Brush over dough
just before baking...so easy!

Grandma's Best Crescent Rolls

Marsha Overholser
Ash Grove, MO

My grandmother's rolls have always been a favorite at our family and church dinners. Grandma used a pie cutter to cut the dough into wedges. These make excellent cinnamon rolls too!

1/4 c. water	1/4 c. oil
1 env. active dry yeast	3/4 t. salt
1/4 c. sugar	3 c. all-purpose flour
3/4 c. warm milk	1/4 c. butter, melted

Heat water until very warm, about 110 to 115 degrees. In a large bowl, dissolve yeast in warm water. Stir in sugar, milk, oil and salt. Add enough flour to make a stiff dough; knead until smooth and elastic. Place dough in a separate greased bowl; turn to coat. Cover and let rise until double in bulk. Punch down dough; divide in half. On a floured surface, roll out each half into a 12-inch circle. Spread melted butter on dough; cut each circle into 12 wedges. Starting at the large end of each wedge, roll up and place in a greased 13"x9" baking pan. Cover and let rise a second time. Bake at 350 degrees for about 20 minutes, or until golden. Makes 2 dozen.

A tiered cake stand is just right for holding a variety of breads, rolls and muffins to serve with dinner.

Delicious Quick Rolls

Ursula Juarez-Wall
Dumfries, VA

My Grandma Bohannon is the most amazing woman I know! Not a single holiday meal passed without Grandma's piping-hot rolls on the table, and for decades she made dozens & dozens of rolls to sell to her neighbors. At ninety-nine years of age, she no longer bakes, so I am glad to share this recipe of hers.

1 c. water	2 T. shortening, melted
1 env. active dry yeast	1 egg, beaten
2 T. sugar	2-1/4 c. all-purpose flour

Heat water until very warm, about 110 to 115 degrees. In a large bowl, dissolve yeast in warm water. Add remaining ingredients; beat until smooth. Cover and let rise until double in size, about 30 to 60 minutes. Punch down. Form dough into 12 balls and place in a greased muffin pan. Cover and let rise again until double, about 30 minutes. Bake at 350 degrees for 15 minutes, or until golden. Makes one dozen.

A loaf of homemade bread is always a welcome gift! To make sure it stays fresh and tasty, let the bread cool completely before wrapping well in plastic wrap or aluminum foil.

Homemade Southern Dumplings

*Lena Butler Smith
Pickerington, OH*

*My grandmother, a southern-raised Native American Indian, made
these dumplings for every holiday for as long as I can remember. It was
an unspoken rule that this is the dish that Mawmaw brings. They're
great to serve over mashed potatoes, rice and chicken. It took me awhile
to convert her recipe from "handfuls & pinches" but I finally got it
worked out. Now, when I make these dumplings, my father feels right
back at home!*

2 c. all-purpose flour
1 c. milk
2 T. butter

salt to taste
32-oz. container chicken or
    beef broth

Combine flour, milk, butter and salt in a large bowl. Mix together by
hand until well blended and dough forms. On a floured surface, roll
dough out 1/2-inch thick. Use a pizza cutter to cut into long noodles,
about 2 inches wide; set aside. In a large stockpot over medium-high
heat, bring broth to a boil. Drop dumplings into boiling broth and cook
for 5 to 7 minutes. Remove when done. Serves 8 to 10.

Add a little whimsy to a buffet table...under an old-fashioned
glass garden cloche, arrange a little bird's nest and
a tiny bluebird from a craft store.

Angel Biscuits

Tara Geiger
Carrollton, TX

It just isn't Sunday dinner without a basket filled with tender biscuits baked from my grandmother's recipe! We've always called them biscuits, but they are really more like a yeast roll.

5 c. all-purpose flour
1/3 c. sugar
1 T. baking powder
2 t. baking soda
2 t. salt

1/2 c. corn oil
2-1/2 c. buttermilk
1/2 c. water
2 envs. active dry yeast

In a large bowl, mix together flour, sugar, baking powder, baking soda and salt; set aside. Mix together oil and buttermilk in a separate bowl; add to flour mixture. Heat water until very warm, about 110 to 115 degrees. Dissolve yeast in warm water; add to mixture and mix thoroughly. Refrigerate overnight in a tightly closed container. With floured hands, pinch off palm-sized pieces of dough; tuck under sides and arrange rolls in a greased 13"x9" baking pan. Cover and let rise 40 minutes to an hour, until double in size. Bake at 450 degrees for 20 minutes, until golden. Makes 2 to 3 dozen rolls.

Keep tiny pots of fresh herbs on the kitchen windowsill...they'll be right at your fingertips for any recipe!

Maravene's Cornbread Gators

Judy Goldthorp
Euless, TX

We've made this cornbread recipe of my mother's for many years. We've always called them "Cornbread Alligators" just for fun...slice open the wedge and the alligator will open his mouth for a bite of butter! This cornbread tastes great with a glass of milk and is a must-have with chili or stew on a chilly day.

1 egg, beaten
1 c. milk
2 T. oil
3/4 c. cornmeal

1 c. all-purpose flour
1/3 c. sugar
1 T. baking powder
1 t. salt

Whisk egg, milk and oil in a bowl; set aside. In a separate bowl, mix remaining ingredients and add to egg mixture. Using a spoon, mix only until moistened; mixture will be lumpy. Pour batter into a greased and floured 9" round cake pan. Bake at 425 degrees for 20 minutes. Cut into wedges. Serves 8.

Treat everyone to honey-pecan butter with warm biscuits or rolls. Simply blend together 1/2 cup butter, 1/2 cup honey and 1/3 cup toasted chopped pecans. Delectable!

Tracy's Bacon Cornbread

Mary Walsh
Valencia, CA

This recipe from Grandma Tracy has been in our family for over fifty years, so you know it has to be good! We love it with bowls of homemade soup.

1 egg, beaten
1 c. milk
1/2 c. bran cereal, shredded or crushed
1 c. yellow cornmeal
1 c. all-purpose flour

2 T. sugar
1-1/2 t. baking powder
Optional: 1/2 t. salt
2 to 3 slices bacon, diced
Garnish: butter

In a large bowl, mix together all ingredients except bacon and butter. Pour into a greased 8"x8" baking pan. Sprinkle bacon over top. Bake at 375 degrees for 30 minutes, or until golden. Cut into squares; serve warm with butter. Makes 8 to 10 servings.

Share silly memories at the next family get-together. Ask everyone to jot down their favorites and toss them in a hat. Pull them out one at a time to read out loud...guaranteed giggles!

Grandmother's Brown Bread

Kathleen Walker
Mountain Center, CA

Serve this hearty old-fashioned bread warm with homemade apple butter...it's the best!

1 c. molasses
2 c. sour milk or buttermilk
2 eggs, beaten
1/4 c. shortening, melted and
cooled
2 c. all-purpose flour

4 c. whole-wheat, graham or
bran flour
1 c. brown sugar, packed
2 t. baking soda
1/2 t. salt

Mix molasses, milk, eggs and shortening in a bowl; set aside. Combine remaining ingredients in a separate large bowl; add molasses mixture and stir until moistened. Pour batter into a greased 9"x5" loaf pan; let stand 20 minutes. Bake at 350 degrees for 45 minutes. Cool on a wire rack. Makes one loaf.

It's fun to bake mini loaves of quick bread in empty food cans...they make great little gifts too! Grease cans well and spoon in batter a bit more than half full. Set cans on a baking sheet and bake at 350 degrees for 25 to 30 minutes, depending on the size of the cans.

Country Wheat Crackers

Jo Ann

*These crisp, hearty homemade crackers are a real treat with
a bowl of hot vegetable soup!*

1 c. whole-wheat flour
1 c. all-purpose flour
1/2 t. baking powder
1/2 t. salt

2 T. butter, diced
1/3 c. water
1 T. whipping cream
Garnish: butter

Mix flours, baking powder and salt in a bowl. Cut in butter with
2 knives until mixture resembles coarse meal. Add water and cream;
stir to form a stiff dough. Pat dough into a 13-inch by 13-inch square
on an ungreased 15"x10" jelly-roll pan. Score into 16 squares; pierce
each square several times with a fork. Bake at 300 degrees for
45 minutes. Cool on pan; break apart and store in an airtight
container. Serve with butter. Makes 16.

Ruth's Swiss Bacon-Onion Dip

*Ruth Cooksey
Plainfield, IN*

A yummy hot appetizer to serve with crackers until dinner is ready.

8-oz. pkg. cream cheese,
softened
1 c. shredded Swiss cheese
1/2 c. mayonnaise
2 T. green onions, chopped

8 slices bacon, crisply cooked
and crumbled
1 c. round buttery crackers,
crushed

Mix cheeses, mayonnaise and onion; spread in a greased
8"x8" baking pan. Top with bacon and cracker crumbs. Bake,
uncovered, at 350 degrees for 15 to 20 minutes, until hot and bubbly.
Makes about 4 cups.

Grammy's Sweet Bread

Susan Rodgers
Mohnton, PA

As a child, I always looked forward to my grandmother bringing a loaf of her sweet bread every Easter and Christmas. She didn't use a written recipe, so one time I asked her how she made it and I wrote it down. It took me several tries until I felt it was as good as Grammy's bread. Thank you, Grammy!

1/2 c. butter, softened
1/2 c. shortening
2 c. sugar
3 eggs, beaten
2 t. vanilla extract
1 c. water
2 envs. active dry yeast

8 c. all-purpose flour
1/2 t. salt
2 c. warm milk
16-oz. pkg. raisins
1/2 c. butter, melted
Garnish: sugar

In a very large bowl, blend together softened butter and shortening. Add sugar, eggs and vanilla, beating well after each addition; set aside. Heat water until very warm, about 110 to 115 degrees. In a cup, add yeast to warm water; stir until dissolved. With a large wooden spoon, gradually stir flour and salt into butter mixture alternately with yeast mixture and warm milk. Mix well; stir in raisins. Turn out dough onto a floured surface. Knead, adding additional flour until dough is no longer sticky. Return dough to bowl. Lightly spray dough with non-stick vegetable spray; cover with wax paper and a tea towel. Let rise 6 to 8 hours or overnight, until double in size. Punch down; divide into 6 equal portions and place in 6 greased 9"x5" loaf pans. Cover and let rise again until rounded, 4 to 6 hours. Drizzle melted butter over loaves; sprinkle with sugar. Bake at 350 degrees for 30 minutes, or until a toothpick tests clean. Cool on wire racks. Makes 6 loaves.

Here's how to tell when rising dough has doubled in size. Press two fingertips 1/2-inch deep into the dough, and then release. If the dent remains, the dough has doubled.

Cinnamon Bread

Dawn Saunders
New Brunswick, Canada

This recipe from my mother is my daughter's very favorite...it is her
only request when she comes home for a visit!

1/2 c. shortening
1 c. sugar
2 eggs, beaten
2 c. all-purpose flour
1 t. baking powder

1/2 t. baking soda
1/4 t. salt
1 c. sour milk or buttermilk
3 T. sugar
1 t. cinnamon

In a large bowl, blend shortening and sugar; stir in eggs and set aside.
In a separate bowl, combine flour, baking powder, baking soda and
salt; add to shortening mixture alternately with milk. Mix sugar and
cinnamon in a cup; set aside. In a greased 9"x5" loaf pan, alternate
4 layers of batter and sugar mixture. Bake at 350 degrees for one
hour. Cool on a wire rack. Makes one loaf.

Choose an older neighbor or friend to "adopt" as a grandparent!
This is so good for your children, especially if their own
grandparents live out of town. As a family you can do little
service projects like washing windows, raking leaves,
or weeding flower beds that will be greatly appreciated.

Peachy Oat Bread

Sharon Velenosi
Stanton, CA

So yummy made with fresh peaches just off the tree! I've also used canned peaches, drained very well.

2 c. whole-wheat flour
1 c. quick-cooking oats, uncooked
3/4 c. sugar
3 T. baking powder
1/2 t. baking soda

1/2 t. salt
1/2 t. cinnamon
2 c. peaches, pitted and chopped
2 eggs, beaten
1 c. milk
1/4 c. oil

In a large bowl, stir together dry ingredients. Add peaches and stir gently to coat; set aside. In a separate bowl, whisk together eggs, milk and oil. Add to peach mixture; stir just until moistened. Pour batter into a greased 9"x5" loaf pan. Bake at 350 degrees for one hour. Cool in pan 10 minutes. Remove from pan and cool completely on a wire rack. Makes one loaf.

Sunday afternoon is a great time to watch sweet and funny old family home movies together. Draw the drapes and scatter plump cushions on the floor for extra seating.
Pass the popcorn, please!

Farmhouse Pumpkin Bread

Brandi Divine
Forney, TX

My Great-Grandmother Mayne used to make this at her home in the country. It is still a family favorite, especially around the holidays.

3-1/2 c. all-purpose flour
3 c. sugar
2 t. baking soda
1-1/2 t. salt
1 t. cinnamon
1 t. nutmeg
1 t. ground ginger

3/4 c. oil
2/3 c. water
4 eggs, beaten
2 c. canned pumpkin
Optional: 1 c. chopped pecans
or walnuts

Combine all ingredients except nuts in a large bowl; mix well. Fold in nuts, if desired. Divide batter into two, 9"x5" loaf pans that have been sprayed with non-stick vegetable spray. Bake at 350 degrees for about 30 minutes. Makes 2 loaves.

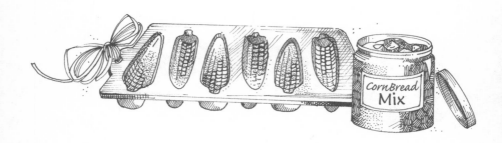

Bake some crisp cornbread sticks. Stir up a corn muffin mix, pour it into a cast-iron cornstick pan and bake according to package directions. So tasty, and little ones love 'em!

Special Zucchini Bread

Tara Geiger
Carrollton, TX

My grandmother had a wonderful fruit & vegetable garden...it was one of my favorite things about her. She would bake this bread for me when I visited her in the summertime. It's yummy served warm with butter or at room temperature with whipped topping!

3 eggs, beaten
2 c. sugar
1 c. oil
1 T. vanilla extract
2 c. zucchini, grated
3 c. all-purpose flour

1/2 t. baking powder
1 t. baking soda
1 T. cinnamon
1 t. salt
1 c. chopped pecans

In a large bowl, beat eggs, sugar, oil, vanilla and zucchini together. Add remaining ingredients in order listed; mix well. Pour batter into 2 greased and floured 8"x4" loaf pans. Bake at 350 degrees for one hour. Makes 2 loaves.

Subtract fat from quick breads, cakes and other baked goods...it's a snap. Just replace some of the oil in the recipe with the same amount of applesauce, puréed prunes or canned pumpkin.

Banana-Nut Bread

Carolyn Ayers
Kent, WA

This scrumptious recipe has been in my family for about seventy-five years. My grandmother lived in Bermuda and made this bread using bananas picked from the banana trees in her yard.

2 c. all-purpose flour
1 c. sugar
1 t. baking soda
1/4 t. salt

1/2 c. canola or safflower oil
2 eggs, beaten
3 very ripe bananas, mashed
1 c. chopped walnuts or pecans

Combine flour, sugar, baking soda and salt in a bowl; mix well and set aside. In a separate large bowl, mix oil and eggs; add bananas. Add flour mixture and mix well; stir in nuts. Pour batter into a greased 9"x5" loaf pan or two, 7"x3" loaf pans. Bake at 350 degrees, 45 minutes for a regular loaf pan or 25 to 30 minutes for 2 smaller pans. Makes one regular loaf or 2 smaller loaves.

Quick breads will have a better flavor if you store them overnight before slicing and serving them.

Apple Pie Bread

Mackenna Ask
Lynnwood, WA

*We especially enjoy this bread at autumn apple-picking time,
but it's wonderful year 'round! It freezes well too.*

3 c. all-purpose flour
1 t. baking powder
1 t. baking soda
1 t. salt
2 t. cinnamon
1 t. nutmeg
1/2 t. ground cloves
3 eggs, beaten

1 c. oil
1-1/4 c. brown sugar, packed
1 c. sugar
1 T. vanilla extract
2 c. Fuji apples, cored, peeled
    and diced
3/4 c. chopped pecans

Sift flour, baking powder, baking soda, salt and spices together in a
bowl; set aside. Beat eggs, oil, sugars and vanilla together in a
separate large bowl. Add flour mixture to egg mixture; beat well. Add
apples and pecans; stir until mixed well. Pour batter into 2 greased
8"x4" loaf pans. Bake at 325 degrees for 40 to 60 minutes, until
a tester inserted in the center comes out clean. Cool pans on a wire
rack for 20 minutes. Turn bread out of pans; cool completely. Makes
2 loaves.

A single vintage quilt patch makes a charming topper for a bread
basket...just stitch it to a large napkin in a matching color.

Raisin Spice Bread

Nancy Neff Bell
Shawnee Mission, KS

This is my grandmother's recipe...it's over a hundred years old! This scrumptious bread is very moist, yet it has no eggs in it.

1 c. shortening
3 c. water
3 c. sugar
16-oz. pkg. raisins
1 t. ground ginger
1 t. ground cloves

1 t. nutmeg
1 t. cinnamon
1/8 t. salt
5 c. all-purpose flour
2 t. baking soda
Optional: chopped nuts to taste

In a large saucepan over medium heat, combine shortening, water, sugar, raisins, spices and salt. Bring to a boil; boil for 5 minutes, stirring occasionally. Remove from heat; cool completely. Add remaining ingredients; mix well. Pour batter into 2 greased and floured 9"x5" loaf pans. Bake at 350 degrees for one hour, or until center tests done. Makes 2 loaves.

Grandma's Best
MAIN DISHES

Mama's Chicken Pot Pie

Jessica Donavant
Forest, VA

This is my grandmother's recipe that she shared with my mama. Mama made this tasty dish quite often when I was growing up. Every time I take a bite, I'm reminded of my childhood, where memories of a winter's day around the dinner table fill me with warmth and comfort.

2 to 3 boneless, skinless chicken breasts
1 onion, sliced
10-3/4 oz. can cream of chicken soup

15-oz. can peas, drained
14-1/2 oz. can sliced carrots, drained
2 eggs, hard-boiled, peeled and chopped

In a large saucepan, cover chicken and onion with water; bring to a boil over high heat. Reduce heat to medium; simmer until chicken is tender, 15 to 20 minutes. Drain, reserving one cup broth. When chicken is cooled, shred. Mix chicken, reserved broth and remaining ingredients together in a large bowl. Pour into a greased 13"x9" baking pan. Spread topping over chicken mixture. Bake, uncovered, at 350 degrees for 45 minutes. Serves 4.

Topping:

1/2 c. butter, softened
1 c. self-rising flour

1 c. milk

In a bowl, stir together all ingredients. Batter will be lumpy.

For juicy, flavorful chicken, cover it with water and simmer gently just until tender, then turn off the heat and let the chicken cool in its own broth.

Country Chicken & Dumplings

Christian Brown
Killeen, TX

*One of those comfort foods that everybody loves! It's extra special
made with homemade broth, but if you're short on time,
a good canned broth is fine.*

3 to 4-lb. roasting chicken
salt and pepper to taste

Garnish: fresh parsley

Roast chicken, covered, in an ungreased roasting pan at 350 degrees
for 1-1/2 hours. Let chicken cool while preparing Supreme Sauce.
Shred chicken; add to simmering sauce. Drop dumplings into sauce
by heaping tablespoonfuls. Cook, covered, 10 to 15 minutes, until
dumplings are firm and puffy. Discard bay leaves. Add salt and
pepper; garnish with parsley. Serves 6.

Supreme Sauce:

2 T. butter
1 T. oil
1/2 c. carrots, peeled and diced
1/2 c. celery, diced
3 cloves garlic, minced

2 bay leaves
5 T. all-purpose flour
6 c. chicken broth
1/4 c. whipping cream

In a Dutch oven, melt butter and oil over medium heat. Add
vegetables and bay leaves. Sauté until soft. Stir in flour; add broth,
one cup at a time, stirring well after each cup. Simmer until thickened;
stir in cream.

Dumplings:

2 c. all-purpose flour
1 T. baking powder
1 t. salt

2 eggs, beaten
3/4 to 1 c. buttermilk, divided

Mix flour, baking powder and salt. Whisk together eggs and 3/4 cup
buttermilk; fold into flour mixture. Stir just until dough forms, adding
a little more buttermilk if needed.

"Secret" Chicken & Cornbread Dressing

Patricia Coffey
Natchitoches, LA

This dressing is everyone's favorite! The "secret ingredient" came about one year when Mama ran out of broth and chicken noodle soup was the closest thing in the pantry. Since then, it is a staple ingredient. My brother and I still make this recipe for our family gatherings, and it is the top request of my brother at the firehouse where he is responsible for heading up holiday meals.

2 8-1/2 oz. pkgs. cornbread
   mix
2 to 4 chicken breasts
1 onion, finely chopped
1 green pepper, finely chopped
1 bunch green onions, chopped
2 stalks celery, chopped
1/4 c. butter

14-1/2 oz. can beef broth
2 10-3/4 oz. cans chicken
   noodle soup
2 eggs, beaten
2 T. dried parsley
1 T. Cajun seasoning
salt and pepper to taste
Optional: 1-1/2 t. dried sage

Bake cornbread according to package directions; cool and crumble. In a saucepan, cover chicken with water; bring to a boil over high heat. Reduce heat; simmer until tender, 20 to 25 minutes. Drain, reserving 1-1/2 cups broth. Cool chicken and shred, discarding bones. In a skillet over medium heat, sauté vegetables in butter until golden; set aside. In a large bowl, mix together cornbread, chicken and vegetable mixture. Add beef broth and reserved chicken broth; stir until mixture is moistened. Add remaining ingredients; mix well. Transfer to a greased 13"x11" baking pan. Bake, covered, at 350 degrees for 45 minutes, or until firm and golden. Serves 4 to 6.

A smiling face is half the meal.

-Latvian proverb

Mrs. Palmer's Fried Chicken

Debbie Donaldson
Andalusia, AL

This recipe brings back precious memories! Every time I fix this recipe I think of being a little girl watching my mama cook. She used the whole chicken, but I use boneless, skinless chicken breasts.

4 to 5 boneless, skinless
   chicken breasts
1 qt. buttermilk
salt and pepper to taste
2 c. self-rising flour
2 t. garlic powder
2 t. dried parsley

2 t. dried thyme
2 t. poultry seasoning
1 t. dried rosemary
1 t. pepper
1 qt. oil
Garnish: chicken gravy or
   sweet-and-sour sauce

Cut chicken into strips, approximately 3 per breast. Place chicken in a large plastic zipping bag; pour buttermilk over chicken. Seal bag and chill for 2 to 3 hours. Drain chicken, discarding buttermilk; season chicken with salt and pepper. In a separate plastic zipping bag, combine flour and seasonings; seal bag and shake to mix well. Add chicken to bag, a few strips at a time; coat thoroughly. Heat oil to 350 degrees in an electric skillet. Carefully place chicken into hot oil; cook until both sides are golden. Drain on paper towels. Serve with chicken gravy or sweet-and-sour sauce. Serves 4.

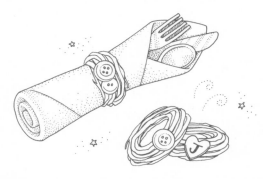

Napkin rings are simple to make. Just sew buttons, charms or fabric yo-yo's onto a 6-inch length of elastic. Stitch the ends together and you're done!

Hearty Chicken Bog

Nicole Manley
Great Lakes, IL

When I was little, I used to go to South Carolina to visit my grandparents for the summer. One year they took me to a town festival featuring this delicious local specialty. Recently I had a craving and decided to try to recreate it my own way...I think I've gotten it pretty close!

1/2 c. butter
1 c. onion, chopped
2 carrots, peeled and diced
2 stalks celery, diced
1 lb. smoked pork sausage, cut in 1-inch pieces
3 lbs. chicken thighs

8 c. water
2 t. Cajun seasoning
2 t. seasoning salt
2 bay leaves
salt and pepper to taste
4 c. instant rice, uncooked

Melt butter in a large stockpot over medium heat. Add onion, carrots and celery; sauté for 2 minutes. Add sausage and chicken; stir. Add water and seasonings; bring to a slow boil. Cover and simmer for 45 minutes. When chicken juices run clear, remove from pot; set aside to cool for a few minutes. Stir in rice; cover and cook over low heat for 10 minutes. Pull chicken from bone; return chicken to stockpot and stir well. Discard bay leaves before serving. Serves 6.

Storytelling time! After dinner, invite family members to share their most treasured family stories. Be sure to save these special moments by capturing them on video.

Aunt Ruth's Mushroom Chicken

Rebecca Wilson
Bessemer City, NC

My Maw-Maw's sister lived about 1-1/2 hours away, which to a kid is quite a distance! We would drive up on a Sunday and this slow-cooker chicken was one of the many things she would fix for us.

6 boneless, skinless chicken
   breasts
10-3/4 oz. can cream of
   mushroom soup

16-oz. container sour cream
1.35-oz. pkg. onion soup mix
cooked rice

Place chicken in a slow cooker. In a bowl, mix together remaining ingredients except rice; spoon over chicken. Cover and cook on high setting for 4 to 6 hours, until chicken is cooked through. Serve with cooked rice. Serves 6.

Barbecue Chicken Marinade

Jodi Blydenburgh
Ilion, NY

This simple recipe has been in my family for years. After a fun-filled day at the lake, Mom would prepare the chicken and Dad would barbecue it. It has become one of my children's favorites as well.

8 boneless, skinless chicken
   breasts
2 c. cider vinegar
3/4 c. oil

1/3 c. salt
1 T. poultry seasoning
1/2 t. pepper

Place chicken in an ungreased 13"x9" glass baking pan; set aside. Combine remaining ingredients in a saucepan; stir well. Bring to a boil over medium heat; cool and pour over chicken. Cover and refrigerate at least 4 hours. Drain; bring marinade to a full boil. Grill chicken over hot coals, turning occasionally and basting with marinade, until juices run clear when pierced, about 30 minutes. Makes 8 servings.

Nanny's Hearty Chicken Noodles

Stephanie White
Sapulpa, OK

My mother-in-law shared this special recipe with me. She brings this dish to every family event. It is delicious...so warm and filling!

3 to 4-lb. roasting chicken
16-oz. pkg. elbow macaroni, uncooked
10-3/4 oz. can cream of chicken soup
10-3/4 oz. can cream of mushroom soup
16-oz. pkg. pasteurized process cheese spread, cubed

Place chicken in a Dutch oven; add water to cover. Bring to a boil over medium-high heat; reduce heat and simmer until chicken juices run clear, 40 to 45 minutes. Remove chicken, reserving broth in Dutch oven; set aside 1-1/2 cups broth. Let chicken cool completely. Add macaroni to broth in Dutch oven; boil until tender, 8 to 10 minutes. While macaroni is cooking, remove bones and skin from chicken. Drain macaroni. Return chicken, macaroni and remaining ingredients to Dutch oven. Cook, uncovered, over medium-low heat for 30 to 40 minutes, stirring often to melt cheese. Stir in some of the reserved broth if mixture becomes too thick. Makes 8 servings.

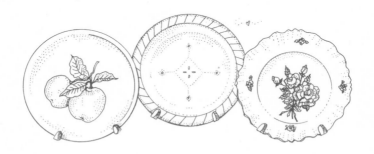

All kinds of table serving pieces can be found at flea markets. Watch for vintage platters, casseroles and jelly-jar glasses to add old-fashioned charm to your dinner table...you may even find a few just like Grandma used to have!

Sunday Chicken Casserole

Arlene Coury
San Antonio, TX

My grandmother would prepare this special dish for holidays and when company was coming. It is the best chicken casserole I have ever tasted...we always made sure we got a helping before it disappeared!

3 to 4 chicken breasts
6-oz. pkg. herb-flavored stuffing
   mix
1/2 c. margarine, melted
10-3/4 oz. can cream of chicken
   soup

16-oz. container sour cream
1/4 c. dill pickle, chopped
1 white onion, chopped

In a large stockpot over medium heat, cover chicken with water. Cook until chicken juices run clear, 20 to 25 minutes. Drain chicken, reserving 1-3/4 cups broth. Let chicken cool. Cut into bite-size pieces, discarding skin and bones; set aside. Toss stuffing mix with melted margarine until moistened. Spread half of stuffing mixture in a lightly greased 11"x8" baking pan; place chicken on top. Blend reserved broth, soup and sour cream until smooth; fold in pickle and onion. Pour over chicken; cover with remaining stuffing mix. Bake, uncovered, at 350 degrees for 20 to 30 minutes, until bubbly. Let stand 10 minutes before serving. Serves 6.

Sometimes it's hard for little ones to wait while dinner's being served. Have crayons, stickers and paper on hand so they can create their own special placemats.

Top-Prize Chicken Casserole

Betty Lou Wright
Hendersonville, TN

This crowd-pleasing dish has graced my family's table for decades. Originally prepared by my mother-in-law, it's been taken many times to potlucks and church suppers. With its creamy sauce and crunchy topping, it's always a hit.

2 to 3 c. cooked chicken, cubed
4 eggs, hard-boiled, peeled and
   chopped
2 c. cooked rice
1-1/2 c. celery, chopped
1 onion, chopped

2 10-3/4 oz. cans cream of
   mushroom soup
1 c. mayonnaise
3-oz. pkg. slivered almonds
2 T. lemon juice
5-oz. can chow mein noodles

Combine all ingredients except chow mein noodles in a large bowl. Mix well; transfer to a greased 3-quart casserole dish. Cover and refrigerate 8 hours to overnight. Bake, uncovered, at 350 degrees for 40 to 45 minutes, until heated through. Top with noodles; return to oven for 5 minutes. Serves 6 to 8.

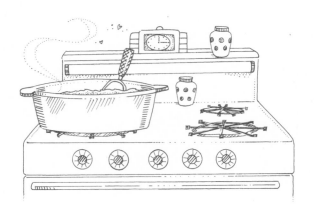

Celebrate Grandparents' Day, September 12, by inviting Grandma & Grandpa to Sunday dinner...let them take it easy while the rest of the family does all the cooking and serving!

Cheddar Chicken Spaghetti

Brenda Dubé
Zanesville, OH

This delicious recipe was given to me by my grandma when I first got married. It's so easy to make! It's a great way to use leftover chicken too.

2 c. cooked chicken, cubed
2 c. shredded Cheddar cheese, divided
10-3/4 oz. can cream of chicken soup
1 c. milk
1/4 t. salt
1/4 t. pepper
Optional: 1 T. diced pimentos
7-oz. pkg. spaghetti, broken up and cooked

In a large bowl, combine chicken, one cup cheese, soup, milk, salt, pepper and pimentos, if using; mix well. Add cooked spaghetti to chicken mixture; toss to coat. Transfer to a greased 13"x9" baking pan; sprinkle with remaining cheese. Bake, uncovered, at 350 degrees for 20 to 25 minutes, or until heated through. Makes 4 to 6 servings.

A shadowbox is perfect for holding all those tiny trinkets collected over the years...charms, button cards, a school pin, souvenir matchboxes, pressed flowers or seashells. Each glance will bring back so many fond memories...such fun to share with family!

Grandma's Turkey à la King

Kelly Alderson
Erie, PA

This rich, creamy dish is so comforting! My grandmother always served it with her homemade puff pastry shells. Now I use convenient bake & serve shells, but you can use split biscuits too.

1/2 c. sliced mushrooms
1/4 c. butter
2 T. all-purpose flour
2 c. chicken broth
1 c. whipping cream

2 c. cooked turkey, cubed
2/3 c. frozen peas, thawed
salt and pepper to taste
6 to 8 frozen puff pastry shells, baked

In a skillet over medium-low heat, sauté mushrooms in butter until tender. Stir in flour until smooth. Whisk in broth; cook and stir until slightly thickened. Stir in remaining ingredients except puff pastry shells. Reduce heat to low; cook until thickened. Serve spooned into shells. Serves 6 to 8.

Serve old-fashioned creamed dishes in crisp toast cups. Trim crusts from bread slices, spread both sides lightly with softened butter and press gently into muffin cups. Bake at 350 degrees for 8 to 10 minutes, until toasted. Fill as desired.

Tuna Noodles Supreme

Gloria Kaufmann
Orrville, OH

A recipe my mother made often when I was a young girl,
over fifty years ago. It's still a favorite of mine...real comfort food.
It is certainly a favorite of my husband too.

3 T. butter
1/4 c. all-purpose flour
2 c. milk
8-oz. pkg. pasteurized process cheese spread, cubed
3 eggs, hard-boiled, peeled and diced

8-oz. pkg. wide egg noodles, cooked
6-oz. can tuna, drained and flaked
1/2 c. sliced mushrooms
salt and pepper to taste
1 c. potato chips, crushed

Melt butter in a large saucepan over medium heat. Stir in flour; cook one minute. Gradually add milk; cook and stir until thickened slightly. Add cheese; stir until melted. Add remaining ingredients except potato chips; mix well. Spoon into a lightly greased 3-quart casserole dish; top with chips. Bake, uncovered, at 350 degrees for 30 minutes, until hot and bubbly. Serves 6.

Try a new topping on a tried & true casserole...sprinkle on seasoned dry bread crumbs, flavored snack cracker crumbs or crispy chow mein noodles. To keep the topping crisp, leave the casserole dish uncovered while it bakes.

Mom's Salmon Patties

Denise Frederick
Climax, NY

*My mom used to make these yummy salmon patties when I was
a child. This recipe brings back such great memories!*

14-3/4 oz. can salmon, drained
    and flaked
1/4 c. onion, finely chopped
1/4 c. cornmeal
1/4 c. all-purpose flour

1 egg, beaten
3 T. mayonnaise
salt and pepper to taste
2 T. oil

Combine all ingredients except oil. Mix until well blended; form into
4 to 5 patties. Heat oil in a skillet over medium heat. Add patties and
cook until golden on each side, turning only once as patties are
fragile. Drain on paper towels. Makes 4 to 5 servings.

Stir up a scrumptious dill
sauce. Blend 1/2 cup sour
cream, one tablespoon Dijon
mustard, one tablespoon
lemon juice and
2 teaspoons chopped fresh
dill. Chill before drizzling
over salmon or tuna patties.

Mawma Nancy's Mac & Cheese

Nancy Carney
Tunica, LA

My granddaughter asks for this casserole at every family get-together.
That's fine with me! The recipe makes a very generous amount and
I usually have most of the ingredients on hand.

5 c. elbow macaroni, cooked
5 T. butter, softened
3 c. milk
2 c. shredded mozzarella cheese
4 c. shredded Cheddar cheese,
   divided

1/2 t. salt
1/2 t. pepper
2 eggs, beaten

In a large bowl, combine cooked macaroni, butter, milk, mozzarella
cheese, 3 cups Cheddar cheese, salt and pepper. Stir in eggs; pour into
a lightly greased 3-quart casserole dish. Cover with aluminum foil
and bake at 350 degrees for 45 minutes. Uncover; sprinkle reserved
Cheddar cheese on top. Bake, uncovered, for an additional 15 minutes,
or until cheese melts. Makes 10 to 12 servings.

When you're hosting the
whole family and are short
on table space, a vintage
wooden ironing board
makes a sturdy sideboard.
Just adjust it to a convenient
height, add a pretty table
runner and set out the
food...come & get it!

Wash-Day Macaroni Casserole

Barb Rudyk
Alberta, Canada

My mother and grandmother used to make this in the 1950s. It was often served on Mondays as this was wash day...I can still remember the wringer washer being in the kitchen and this tomato-macaroni casserole in the oven. It's just plain good!

2 T. margarine
2 T. all-purpose flour
1-1/2 c. milk
1 c. elbow macaroni, cooked
15-oz. can diced tomatoes

1/2 c. celery, diced
3 T. onion, chopped
3/4 c. shredded Cheddar cheese, divided

Melt margarine in a saucepan over medium heat. Stir in flour; cook and stir for one minute. Gradually add milk; cook and stir until thickened. Set aside. Combine cooked macaroni, undrained tomatoes, celery, onion and 1/2 cup cheese; pour into a greased 1-1/2 quart casserole dish. Add margarine mixture and toss to coat; sprinkle with remaining cheese. Bake, uncovered, at 350 degrees for 30 minutes, or until hot and bubbly. Serves 4.

Take a little time to share family traditions with your kids or grandkids! A cherished family recipe can be a great conversation starter at dinner.

Grandma Knorberg's Pork Chop Casserole

Shirl Parsons
Cape Carteret, NC

This is the ultimate in comfort food!

6 pork chops, trimmed
salt and pepper to taste
1/8 t. dried sage
10-3/4 oz. can cream of
  mushroom soup

1/2 c. water
1 c. carrots, peeled and sliced
1/2 c. celery, sliced

Arrange pork chops in an ungreased 13"x9" baking pan; sprinkle with salt, pepper and sage. Mix remaining ingredients; spoon over chops. Bake, covered, at 350 degrees for one hour. Makes 6 servings.

If you have children just learning to set the table, have them draw a "proper" place setting on a big sheet of paper. Laminate their artwork and they'll have a special placemat that helps them put the silverware in the right place.

Pork Chop Delight

*Janet Vaughn
Darien, IL*

This is a recipe passed down from my mother. She was a great cook though she didn't even like to cook! This recipe is still a favorite all these years later. They literally melt in your mouth...thanks, Mom!

8 boneless thin-sliced pork
   chops
1/3 c. water

1/2 c. chili sauce, divided
1-1/2 c. brown sugar, packed

Place pork chops in an ungreased 13"x9" baking pan. Add water to bottom of pan to prevent sticking. Top each pork chop with a tablespoon of chili sauce; sprinkle brown sugar over all. Bake, uncovered, at 325 degrees for one hour; do not turn pork chops over. Makes 8 servings.

I am most thankful for...

Start a Sunday dinner tradition! Lay a blank card on each dinner plate and invite family & friends to write down what they are most thankful for today. Afterward, bind the cards together with a ribbon to create a sweet gratitude book.

Mama's Sunday Pork Chops

Kathleen Rampy
Midlothian, TX

My mother would bring over this delicious dish
whenever I came home with a new baby.

2 eggs, beaten
2 sleeves saltine crackers,
  crushed
6 to 8 pork loin or butterfly
  chops
2 T. oil

2 10-3/4 oz. cans cream of
  mushroom soup
1 c. water
1/3 c. onion, chopped
salt and pepper to taste

Place beaten eggs in a shallow bowl; add cracker crumbs to a separate shallow bowl and set aside. In a skillet over medium heat, brown pork chops in oil. Drain; allow to cool slightly. Dip pork chops in eggs, then in cracker crumbs to coat. Arrange pork chops in a Dutch oven. Spoon soup over pork chops; pour water over soup. Sprinkle with onion, salt and pepper. Bake, uncovered, at 350 degrees for 1-1/2 hours. Serves 6 to 8.

Stir some seasoned salt and coarsely ground pepper into flour,
then fill a big shaker to keep by the side of the stove.
So handy to sprinkle on meat for pan-frying!

Brown Sugar Ham Loaf

Libby Hiatt
Mitchellville, IA

This yummy recipe was my mother's. Our Methodist church has a "Dinner Day Potluck" the first Sunday of every month. I always take this ham loaf. People really seem to enjoy it!

2 lbs. smoked ham, ground
1-1/2 lbs. ground pork
1 c. saltine cracker crumbs

2 eggs, beaten
1 c. milk

Combine all ingredients in a large bowl; mix well. Form into 2 loaves; place in 2 greased 9"x5" loaf pans. Bake, uncovered, at 350 degrees for one hour. Baste with Brown Sugar Sauce during the last 30 minutes of baking. Makes 2 ham loaves; each serves 8.

Brown Sugar Sauce:

1 c. brown sugar, packed
1/4 c. cider vinegar

1/2 c. water
1 t. mustard

Mix ingredients until smooth.

Just for fun, use a special tablecloth and ask family members, friends and special visitors to sign it with fabric markers.

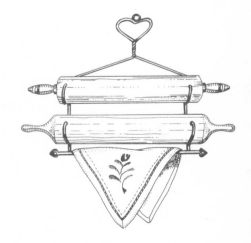

Farmstyle Ham & Gravy

Rochelle Degryse
Bryan, OH

This was my grandma's recipe. She and Grandpa raised eleven children on their farm. All of my aunts and uncles made ham this way too. Our family likes to ladle the gravy over ham and mashed potatoes...a real stick-to-your-ribs meal! This can also be made in a large slow cooker. Cover and cook on low setting for 6 to 8 hours.

8 to 10-lb. fully-cooked ham,
    boneless or bone-in
whole cloves to taste

3/4 c. brown sugar, packed
2 12-oz. cans ginger ale

Place ham in an ungreased roasting pan. Insert cloves, a few inches apart, on top and partway down sides of ham. Pat brown sugar onto top and sides of ham. Gently pour ginger ale over ham without rinsing off all the brown sugar. Pour remaining ginger ale into roasting pan. Cover and bake at 325 degrees for one to 1-1/2 hours, until a meat thermometer inserted in center of ham reads 140 degrees. Remove ham to a serving platter, reserving drippings. Let ham stand for 5 to 10 minutes before slicing. Serve with Pan Gravy. Serves 8 to 10.

Pan Gravy:

reserved pan drippings
1/2 c. cornstarch

1 c. cold water

Transfer drippings from roasting pan to a saucepan; bring to a boil over medium heat. Whisk together cornstarch and water. Slowly add mixture to pan drippings, whisking well. Cook and stir until gravy thickens. Use more or less of cornstarch mixture, depending upon quantity of drippings.

Ham Steak & Apples Skillet

Gail Prather
Hastings, NE

My grandmother's old black cast-iron skillet brings back wonderful memories of the delicious things she used to make in it. I seek out scrumptious skillet recipes just so I can use Grandma's old skillet... this one has become a real favorite at our house!

3 T. butter
1/2 c. brown sugar, packed
1 T. Dijon mustard

2 c. apples, cored and diced
2 1-lb. bone-in ham steaks

Melt butter in a large skillet over medium heat. Add brown sugar and mustard; bring to a simmer. Add apples; cover and simmer for 5 minutes. Top apples with ham steaks. Cover with a lid; simmer for about 10 minutes more, until apples are tender. Remove ham to a platter and cut into serving-size pieces. Top ham with apples and sauce. Makes 6 servings.

We all remember that happy feeling as kids when a party invitation arrived in the mail! Ask a few family friends to Sunday dinner and mail out written invitations to them...your grown-up friends will love it!

Cheesy Ham Potatoes

Tricia Roberson
King George, VA

Whenever I need cheering up, I make this recipe. I think back to Kansas and a wintery day and see myself rubbing a spot in the frost on the window to see outside. It always smelled like home at Grandma's, and that's what I taste when I eat this comforting dish.

30-oz. pkg. frozen diced
    potatoes
10-3/4 oz. can cream of potato
    soup
10-3/4 oz. can cream of celery
    soup
8-oz. container sour cream

1 c. milk
1 lb. cooked ham, diced
2 green onions, chopped
salt and pepper to taste
8-oz. pkg. shredded sharp
    Cheddar cheese, divided

In a large bowl, combine all ingredients, reserving one cup cheese for topping. Bake, covered, at 350 degrees for one hour. Sprinkle reserved cheese on top. Cook, uncovered, for an additional 30 minutes. Let stand for a few minutes before serving. Serves 8.

Frame a piece of old-fashioned lace and some vintage buttons from your grandmother's sewing box. What a sweet remembrance!

Grandma's Creole Beef

Terri Lotz-Ganley
South Euclid, OH

When I was a little girl, my mom had her own catering business that she ran from our home. Mom handed down her passion for cooking to me, and this recipe from her own mother was one of the first things she taught me to cook. For variety, use ground pork instead of beef.

3 lbs. ground beef
3/4 c. onion, minced
2 t. garlic, minced
8-oz. can tomato sauce
6-oz. can tomato paste
1/4 c. catsup

1 c. water
2 T. onion powder
16-oz. pkg. elbow macaroni,
  uncooked
salt and pepper to taste

Brown beef in a large saucepan over medium heat; drain. Add remaining ingredients except macaroni, salt and pepper; stir until well mixed. Cover and simmer for 30 minutes, stirring occasionally. While sauce is simmering, cook macaroni according to package directions; drain. Place cooked macaroni in a large serving bowl. Pour sauce over macaroni and mix well. Add salt and pepper to taste. Serves 8.

Decorate your dining room table with a simple table runner for each season. There are so many charming seasonal print fabrics available! You'll just need a couple of yards of fabric for a runner. Rick-rack edging and a tassel at each end are nice finishing touches.

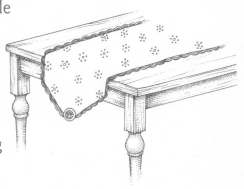

Red Dumplings

Elizabeth Ong
Porter, TX

My family loves this biscuit-topped skillet dinner! I can remember eating it when I was very little and my grandmother fixed it for us. Mama wrote on the recipe card that it was from 1950.

1 lb. ground beef
1/2 lb. ground pork sausage
2 green peppers, sliced into
 rings
1 onion, sliced and separated
 into rings

46-oz. can cocktail vegetable
 juice
1 to 2 12-oz. cans refrigerated
 biscuits, depending on
 skillet size
salt and pepper to taste

Mix beef and sausage in a bowl; form into 4 patties. Brown patties in a skillet over medium heat. Drain; add green peppers and onion to skillet on top of patties. Pour in vegetable juice to completely cover patties. Bring to a boil; cover and reduce heat to a simmer for 30 minutes. Arrange enough biscuits to cover mixture in skillet; spoon juice over biscuits. Cover and cook an additional 10 minutes, or until biscuits are done. Add salt and pepper as desired. Serves 4.

Place a pair of whimsical salt & pepper shakers on the dining room table. With so many clever designs, from cows and pigs to kissing couples, they're fun for everyone!

Baba's Meatballs

Carol Geyer
Port Charlotte, FL

This is a recipe from my Baba, as we called my grandmother. She knew all the old Slovakian ways of making food stretch.

3 slices white bread
3 lbs. ground beef
2 eggs, beaten
1 onion, chopped
1/4 c. fresh parsley, chopped
1 c. milk

5 potatoes, peeled and halved
5 stalks celery, halved
 lengthwise
2 to 3 T. margarine, thinly sliced
pepper to taste

Let bread slices stand at room temperature for 2 hours, until slightly dry. Combine beef, eggs, onion and parsley in a large bowl; set aside. Tear bread into bite-size pieces. Dip bread in milk and add to beef mixture, blending well. Form into baseball-size balls; place in an ungreased roasting pan. Add potatoes; place celery across meatballs and potatoes. Dot meatballs with margarine; sprinkle with pepper. Bake, covered, at 350 degrees for 2 hours, or until meatballs are cooked through and vegetables are tender. Serves 4 to 6.

If you're putting together a family cookbook, be sure to ask your kids about their best-liked foods. You may find there are special favorites that you weren't even aware of!

Grandma B's Pig in a Blanket

Krystal Henry
Nashville, IL

This is one of my favorite comfort foods of all time...an easy take on stuffed cabbage rolls that makes the house smell delicious. Going to Grandma's farm on the weekends was always my favorite thing to do...fishing, climbing trees, picking veggies from the garden, and just running around in the fresh country air, followed by a wonderful meal cooked by Grandma.

1-1/2 lbs. ground beef
1 onion, diced
2 cloves garlic, diced
salt and pepper to taste

2 28-oz. cans diced tomatoes
1 c. instant rice, uncooked
1 head cabbage, shredded
2 c. tomato juice, divided

In a skillet over medium heat, brown beef with onion, garlic, salt and pepper. Drain and set aside. Combine undrained tomatoes and rice. Add beef mixture and mix well; transfer to a greased 13"x9" baking pan. Place shredded cabbage on top. Drizzle one cup of tomato juice over cabbage. Bake, uncovered, at 350 degrees for 20 minutes; add remaining tomato juice if needed. Cover with aluminum foil. Bake an additional hour, or until rice and cabbage are tender. Serves 6 to 8.

Be sure to have enough plastic containers on hand to send everyone home with leftovers...if there are any!

Mama's Meatloaf

Maxine Blakely
Seneca, SC

My mother has made this recipe for years. Once you've tried it, you won't want to make any other meatloaf! The glaze is what makes the meatloaf so delicious.

1-1/2 lbs. ground beef
2 eggs, beaten
3/4 c. milk
2/3 c. saltine cracker crumbs
salt and pepper to taste

Optional: 2 t. onion, chopped
1/4 c. catsup
2 t. brown sugar, packed
1 t. mustard
1 T. lemon juice

In a large bowl, mix together beef, eggs, milk, cracker crumbs, salt, pepper and onion, if using. Form into a loaf and place in an ungreased 9"x5" loaf pan. Bake, covered, at 350 degrees for 45 minutes. Mix remaining ingredients; spread over meatloaf. Bake, uncovered, an additional 15 minutes. Serves 6 to 8.

Mashed potatoes are the perfect side dish for savory meatloaf. Try a delicious secret the next time you make the potatoes... substitute equal parts chicken broth and cream for the milk in any favorite recipe.

Nana's Hamburg Pie

Christine Walker
Norwell, MA

One Christmas, my grandmother made me a handwritten cookbook. Each recipe has her little notes about changes she made, which ones were my grandfather's favorites and which ones were crowd-pleasers. It's fun to make the recipes from her book...they bring back so many memories of family gatherings. This is one of my favorites!

1 onion, chopped
2 to 3 t. oil
1 lb. ground beef
3/4 t. salt
1/8 t. pepper

2 c. green beans
10-3/4 oz. can tomato soup
Optional: shredded Cheddar
 cheese

In a skillet over medium heat, cook onion in oil until tender. Add beef, salt and pepper; brown lightly and drain. Add green beans and soup; mix well. Spoon into a greased 1-1/2 quart casserole dish. Drop Potato Fluff Topping in mounds over beef mixture. If desired, sprinkle cheese over topping. Bake, uncovered, at 350 degrees for 25 to 30 minutes. Serves 6.

Potato Fluff Topping:

5 potatoes, peeled and cooked
1/2 c. warm milk

1 egg, beaten
salt and pepper to taste

While still warm, mash potatoes with remaining ingredients.

Mimi's Spanish Rice

Emily Borup
Honolulu, HI

Three generations of my family have enjoyed my grandmother's Spanish Rice...even after her passing, my grandfather continues to make it for the family. It is simple to make and full of flavor.

1 lb. ground beef, browned
   and drained
1 onion, chopped
1 t. garlic powder
1 t. seasoned salt
1/2 t. salt
1/4 t. pepper
3 c. instant rice, uncooked

3 c. beef broth
10 slices bacon, crisply cooked
   and crumbled
14-1/2 oz. can diced tomatoes
3 to 4 c. cocktail vegetable juice
bread and butter or warm flour
   tortillas

In a skillet over medium heat, brown beef with onion and seasonings; drain. Prepare rice according to package directions, substituting broth for water. In a greased 13"x9" baking pan, combine beef mixture, rice, bacon and undrained tomatoes. Add vegetable juice to rice mixture, a little at a time, just to moisten. Bake, uncovered, at 350 degrees for 30 minutes, or until heated through. Serve with bread and butter or warm tortillas. Serves 6.

When preparing a favorite casserole, it's easy to make a double batch. After baking, let the extra casserole cool, wrap well and tuck it in the freezer...ready to share with a new mother, carry to a potluck or reheat on a busy night at home.

Grandma's Hot Dish

Christine Horjus
Hebron, IN

As far back as I can remember, we've had this hearty slow-cooked ground beef dish of my grandmother's at every Christmas gathering. She learned this recipe from her Norwegian sisters while growing up in Minnesota. Grandma is ninety-three now and since she no longer lives on her own, my sister and I are carrying on the tradition.

3 lbs. ground beef, browned and drained
3 15-oz. cans chili without beans
2 10-3/4 oz. cans cream of mushroom soup
2 10-3/4 oz. cans Cheddar cheese soup
1 onion, diced
16-oz. pkg. rotini pasta, cooked

In a 6-quart slow cooker, combine all ingredients except rotini. Cover and cook on high setting for a total of 2 hours. Add cooked rotini to slow cooker 30 minutes before serving, stirring to mix. Cover and cook for an additional 30 minutes. Makes 8 servings.

Getting together with family & friends for a country-style potluck? Slow cookers are ideal. Tote them along filled with your favorite spiced cider, casserole, roast or fruit cobbler...scrumptious!

Moo-Cow Casserole

Anee Turner
Magnolia, AR

This recipe is special to me because of my grandmother, whom I called Maw. She always cooked a hot lunch for my grandfather and this is one of her delicious "made-up" recipes.

1-1/2 lbs. ground beef
1 onion, chopped
1 green pepper, chopped
11-oz. can corn, drained
1 c. shredded Cheddar cheese
1 egg, beaten
1/3 c. catsup
1/4 c. milk

1 jalapeño pepper, chopped
2 T. Worcestershire sauce
garlic salt, salt and pepper
   to taste
2 c. soft bread, torn into small
   pieces and divided
2 to 3 T. butter, melted

In a skillet over medium heat, sauté beef, onion and green pepper; drain. In a large bowl, mix together remaining ingredients except one cup bread pieces and butter. Add beef mixture to corn mixture; pour into a lightly greased 3-quart casserole dish. Top casserole with reserved bread; drizzle with melted butter. Bake, uncovered, at 350 degrees for 30 minutes, or until bread is toasted. Serves 6.

Handwritten menus lend a personal touch to any table. Cut pretty scrapbooking paper to fit a picture frame and write on the details with a colored marker.

Granny's Winter Dinner

Martha-Ann Daly
Flagstaff, AZ

My grandmother made this simple oven stew for us on cold winter nights. It has continued to be a family favorite for many years. With a crisp green salad and a light dessert, it's a complete meal.

1 lb. stew beef, cubed
2 T. shortening
1 c. water
4-oz. jar button mushrooms
3 potatoes, peeled and sliced

3/4 c. sour cream
10-3/4 oz. can cream of
   mushroom soup
3/4 c. milk
1 c. shredded Cheddar cheese

In a large, heavy saucepan, brown beef in shortening over medium heat. Drain; add water and mushrooms with liquid. Reduce heat to low; cover and simmer for 2 hours. Transfer beef mixture to an ungreased 13"x9" baking pan; arrange potatoes on top. In a separate bowl, mix sour cream, soup and milk; spoon over potatoes. Sprinkle cheese on top. Bake, uncovered, at 350 degrees for 1-1/2 hours. Serves 4 to 6.

Create a family tradition of honoring birthdays, good marks at school and other milestones. Look for a dinner plate that says "You Are Special" or simply choose a brightly colored plate that stands out from the rest of your dinnerware.

Country Goulash

Amy Woods
Collinsville, TX

*My Granny Roberts used to place this mixture in a casserole dish
and bake it with homemade biscuits on top. Yum!*

1 lb. lean ground beef
1 clove garlic, minced
1 onion, chopped
1 green pepper, chopped
16-oz. pkg. tri-color rotini
  pasta, cooked

14-oz. can diced tomatoes,
  drained
16-oz. can pinto beans, drained
  and rinsed
3 T. chili powder
1/2 t. salt

In a large saucepan over medium heat, brown beef with garlic, onion
and pepper; drain. Add cooked pasta and remaining ingredients; toss
to coat. Heat through over low heat. Serves 4 to 6.

Hosting a reunion dinner? Ask family members to
each bring a baby photo. Have a contest...the first person
to guess who's who gets a prize!

Greek Beef Roast

Joanna Karpinski
Hudson, OH

My Yiayia (grandmother) Stella brought this recipe with her from Greece in the 1920s. It was, and is, a family favorite for Sunday visits, especially when the weather turns cold. Put it in the oven early in the day and enjoy a scrumptious supper...it makes the whole house smell so delicious! We serve this with tiny orzo or rosamarina pasta cooked with beef broth and a cinnamon stick. Yum!

3 to 4-lb. beef chuck roast,
   trimmed
2 T. oil
14-1/2 oz. can beef broth

3/8 c. tomato paste
4 4-inch cinnamon sticks
salt and pepper to taste

In a hot skillet over medium-high heat, brown roast in oil on all sides. Place roast in an ungreased roasting pan; pour broth over roast. Add tomato paste to broth, mashing it into the broth with the back of a spoon. Add cinnamon sticks to broth. Season roast with salt and pepper. Cover with wax paper, then tightly with aluminum foil. Bake at 325 degrees for 4 to 5 hours, until fork-tender. Serves 6 to 8.

Bake potatoes in the microwave...it's quick & easy. Pierce baking potatoes with a fork and place in microwave, 4 to 5 at a time. Microwave on high for 2 minutes, turn potatoes over and microwave another 2 to 3 minutes.

Nanny's Famous Beef Stroganoff

Sandy Lakeman
Algonquin, IL

Saucy beef and noodles...so good on a chilly day!

1/2 lb. sliced mushrooms
1 onion, chopped
1/4 c. butter, divided
2 lbs. beef round steak, cut into
    2-1/2 inch strips
1/4 to 1/2 c. all-purpose flour

10-1/2 oz. can beef broth
3/4 c. water
1 t. salt
8-oz. container sour cream
cooked egg noodles

In a large skillet over medium heat, sauté mushrooms and onion in 2 tablespoons butter. Remove mixture to a bowl and set aside. Toss beef in flour, coating thoroughly. Add remaining butter to skillet and brown beef; add broth, water and salt. Reduce heat. Cover and simmer until beef is tender, stirring occasionally, about 1-1/2 hours. Add mushroom mixture and sour cream; heat through. Serve over cooked noodles. Serves 6.

A no-fuss way to cook egg noodles...bring water to a rolling boil, then turn off heat. Add noodles; cover and let stand for 20 minutes, stirring twice. Perfect!

Boneless Birds

Briana Branchflower
Portland, OR

This recipe was first made by my great-grandmother from Germany, then by my grandmother in Chicago, then fixed for special occasions by my mother here in Portland. The aroma that filled our kitchen always let my sister and me know we were celebrating something wonderful.

5 lbs. beef round steak, cut into
   16 pieces
1/2 c. mustard
16-oz. pkg. bacon, halved
1 onion, halved and sliced
12 thin dill pickle wedges

2 T. oil
1/2 c. dill pickle juice
1/4 c. all-purpose flour
1 c. cold water
salt and pepper to taste
mashed potatoes

Pound out steak pieces to 1/4-inch thick. Spread each piece generously with mustard; top each piece with 1/2 slice uncooked bacon, an onion slice and a dill pickle wedge. Roll up; secure with a wooden toothpick. Heat oil in a large, heavy saucepan over high heat. Brown steak rolls, reserving drippings in saucepan. When all of the rolls are browned, add water just to cover. Add remaining onion, pickle and pickle juice to saucepan. Bring to a boil; reduce to a simmer. Cover; cook 2 to 3 hours, until fork-tender. Remove steak rolls to a serving plate and cover, reserving drippings. To make gravy, mix flour and water together to form a paste. Add to hot drippings in pan over medium-high heat, cooking and stirring until thickened. Stir in salt and pepper to taste. Serve steak rolls with mashed potatoes and gravy. Serves 8.

Sweet little servings of butter are easy to make with
a melon baller...a charming change from butter pats and
an easy make-ahead.

Grandma Ruth's Stuffed Hot Dogs
Janelle Hofstetter
Dalton, OH

My husband's grandmother started making this recipe as a young working woman in the late 1930s or early 1940s and then as her family grew. Now her great-grandchildren are enjoying them too!

8 hot dogs
6-oz. pkg. stuffing mix,
    prepared

2 10-3/4-oz. cans tomato soup

Slice hot dogs down the middle but do not cut through. Place hot dogs, cut-side up, in a greased 13"x9" baking pan. Spoon prepared stuffing into each hot dog; top with soup. Bake, uncovered, at 350 degrees for 30 minutes, or until heated through. Serves 8.

Red-Hots & Noodles
Jessica Mihos
Morrisville, PA

A recipe that my grandmother made and is still talked about to this day! We just found it again in her recipe box. It's super-simple but really yummy...give it a try!

1/2 c. catsup
1/2 c. water
1/4 c. chili sauce
1 T. Worcestershire sauce
1 T. brown sugar, packed
1 t. lemon juice

1/4 t. chili powder
1/4 t. salt
8 hot dogs, cut into bite-size
    pieces
cooked egg noodles

In a large saucepan, combine all ingredients except hot dogs and noodles; stir well. Bring to a boil over medium heat; reduce heat and simmer for 3 minutes. Add hot dogs; heat through. Serve over cooked noodles. Serves 6 to 8.

Sunday Gravy for Pasta

Annette Mullan
North Arlington, NJ

Growing up in a big Italian family, every Sunday was pasta day. Early Sunday morning Mom would get up and make the sauce, which we call gravy. The smells throughout the house would be amazing. It still isn't Sunday without this big pot of gravy. Add some crusty Italian bread and a tossed salad, and dinner is served!

1 T. olive oil
1/4 onion, finely chopped
1 clove garlic, finely chopped
2 14-1/2 oz. cans crushed
   tomatoes
28-oz. can tomato purée
6-oz. can tomato paste
1-1/2 c. water
1-1/2 t. onion powder

1-1/2 t. garlic powder
1-1/2 t. dried basil
salt to taste
Optional: 1/8 t. red pepper
   flakes
Optional: sweet Italian pork
   sausage, browned, to taste
cooked spaghetti

Heat oil in a large soup pot over medium-high heat. Add onion and garlic; sauté until onion is translucent. Add tomatoes, tomato purée, tomato paste and water. Stir in seasonings and red pepper flakes, if desired. Add browned sausage, if desired. Partially cover pot; reduce heat to low. Simmer for 2 to 2-1/2 hours, stirring occasionally. Serve gravy over spaghetti. Serves 4 to 6.

An instant appetizer...set out a warm loaf of Italian bread and little dishes of olive oil sprinkled with Italian seasoning for dipping.

Savory Salisbury Steak

Dee Dee Plzak
Westmont, IL

My mother shared this recipe with me. For some reason, my kids like it better when Grandma cooks it and always ask for "her" Salisbury steak instead of mine...it must be the dish she serves it in!

10-3/4 oz. can golden
    mushroom soup, divided
1/3 c. water
1-1/2 lbs. lean ground beef
1 onion, finely chopped

1/2 c. bread crumbs
1 egg, beaten
1/2 t. salt
1/8 t. pepper

In a small bowl, mix 3/4 cup soup and water; set aside. In a separate bowl, mix remaining soup and other ingredients. Form into small patties; arrange in a single layer in a greased 13"x9" baking pan. Bake, uncovered, at 350 degrees for 30 minutes. Drain; spoon reserved soup mixture over patties. Bake, uncovered, an additional 10 to 12 minutes. Serves 4 to 6.

A lovely dinner table centerpiece in a snap! Set a short pillar candle on a food can inside a clear glass punch bowl, then fill the bowl with shiny red or green apples.

SCRUMPTIOUS Desserts

Chloe's Strawberry Pie

Rachel Boyd
Defiance, OH

This luscious pie is my great-grandma's recipe that has been handed down in our family. It is our most requested first-of-summer pie...just when strawberries are in season!

3 c. strawberries, hulled
9-inch pie crust, baked
1 c. sugar
3 T. cornstarch

1 c. water
2 T. corn syrup
2 T. strawberry gelatin mix

Slice 2 cups strawberries; chop remaining strawberries and set aside. Arrange sliced strawberries in baked pie crust; set aside. In a saucepan over medium-low heat, mix together sugar, cornstarch, water and corn syrup. Add reserved chopped strawberries; cook until thickened. Stir in dry gelatin mix; cool. Pour mixture into pie crust; cover and chill until firm. Makes 8 servings.

Oh-So-Easy Pie Crust

Kate Scott
Mulberry, IN

This is an easy crust to handle and can be re-rolled without becoming tough. The recipe came from a cookbook my granny gave me, from the small-town church she and my mother attend.

1-1/4 c. shortening
3 c. all-purpose flour
1 t. salt

1 egg, beaten
5 T. water
1 T. vinegar

In a bowl, cut shortening into flour and salt. In a separate bowl, whisk egg, water and vinegar; pour into flour mixture. Blend with a spoon just until moistened. Roll out dough on a floured surface; divide into 2 parts. Use immediately or wrap and refrigerate up to 2 weeks before using. Makes two, 9-inch pie crusts.

Granny's Shoo-Fly Pie

Kristi Boyle
Easton, MD

My children are so happy when we go to Granny's house and she has just pulled a warm shoo-fly pie out of the oven. It's amazing that such a yummy pie can be made from these simple ingredients!

1 c. molasses
1/2 c. brown sugar, packed
3 eggs, beaten

1 t. baking soda
1 c. hot water
9-inch pie crust

Mix together all ingredients except crust. Pour half the mixture into unbaked pie crust; spread 1/4 of Crumb Topping over top. Pour in remaining molasses mixture; add remaining topping. Bake at 400 degrees for 10 minutes. Reduce oven to 375 degrees; bake an additional 50 minutes. Cool completely before slicing. Serves 8.

Crumb Topping:

2-1/2 c. all-purpose flour
1 c. brown sugar, packed

1/2 c. shortening

Mix all ingredients until crumbly.

For a scrumptious dessert in a jiffy, make an ice cream pie! Soften two pints of your favorite ice cream and spread in a graham cracker crust, then freeze. Garnish with whipped topping and cookie crumbs or fresh berries.

Old-Fashioned Sugar Cream Pie

Brenda Huey
Geneva, IN

This was my Grandma Cline's famous pie recipe. It is so good! She's gone now, but my mother and I use this recipe in our bakery.

1/2 c. sugar
1/2 c. brown sugar, packed
2 T. all-purpose flour

1 c. whipping cream
9-inch pie crust

Whisk together sugars, flour and cream; pour into unbaked pie crust. Bake at 350 degrees for 30 to 40 minutes, until top is bubbly. Cool completely before slicing. Serves 8.

Mom's No-Fail Pie Pastry

Richelle Leck
Ontario, Canada

A recipe handed down from my grandmother to my mother, then to me. My grandparents came from England, so I suppose it came from there generations back.

5 c. all-purpose flour
1 t. baking powder
1/2 t. salt

2 c. lard or shortening
1 egg, beaten
1 t. vinegar

In a large bowl, combine flour, baking powder, salt and lard or shortening; mix until well blended. Place egg and vinegar in a measuring cup; add warm water until it measures one cup total. Mix lightly. Make a well in middle of flour mixture; pour in egg mixture. Stir until pastry is smooth. Divide into 4 equal parts and roll out on a floured surface. Makes four, 9-inch pie crusts.

An old-time treat for the kids! Roll out scraps of pie dough, sprinkle with cinnamon-sugar and bake at 350 degrees for about 10 minutes, or until golden.

Nan's Chocolate Pie

Becky Ladd
Delaware, OH

The most delicious chocolate pie ever! This recipe belonged to my grandmother. She was such a wonderful cook and an excellent seamstress too, who made a lot of my older sister's and my clothes.

1 c. sugar
3 T. cornstarch
1/3 c. baking cocoa
1/4 t. salt
1-1/2 c. milk
3 egg yolks, beaten

1/4 c. butter
1 t. vanilla extract
1/2 t. almond extract
9-inch pie crust, baked
Garnish: whipped cream, grated
chocolate

In a saucepan, combine sugar, cornstarch, cocoa and salt; gradually stir in milk. Cook and stir over medium-high heat until bubbly. Cook and stir an additional 2 minutes; remove from heat. Stir a small amount of hot mixture into egg yolks. Immediately add yolk mixture to saucepan and cook 2 minutes over low heat, stirring constantly. Remove from heat; add butter and extracts. Stir until smooth. Pour into baked pie crust. Cool in refrigerator; garnish with whipped cream and grated chocolate. Serves 8.

Adding chocolate curls dresses up any homemade dessert and they're a snap to make...just pull a vegetable peeler across a chocolate bar.

Grandma Katie's Glacé Pie

Suzy Brugger Kanode
Weyers Cave, VA

I can remember picking the blueberries for this pie with my grandma and mother, then dividing them up among us. This is by far the most scrumptious pie I make...everywhere I take it, everyone raves and asks for the recipe!

4 c. blueberries, divided
1 c. water, divided
1 c. sugar

3 T. cornstarch
9-inch pie crust, baked

In a saucepan over low heat, combine one cup blueberries and 2/3 cup water. Simmer for about 5 minutes; stir. Add sugar, cornstarch and remaining water; boil one minute, stirring constantly. Cool slightly. Put 2 cups blueberries into baked pie crust. Pour cooked mixture over blueberries. Top with remaining blueberries. Cover and chill until serving time. Makes 8 servings.

After Sunday dinner, set up old-fashioned games like
badminton and croquet in the backyard...fun for all ages!
Indoors, try favorite board games. Everyone is sure
to have a great time.

Simple Crumb Cake

Mary Anne Acquisto
Pocono Summit, PA

*This recipe was handed down through the family from my
great-grandmother. It's scrumptious and simple to make.*

18-1/2 oz. pkg. yellow or
   white cake mix
2/3 c. milk

2/3 c. oil
4 eggs, beaten
Garnish: powdered sugar

Mix together dry cake mix, milk, oil and eggs. Spread batter in a
greased 13"x9" baking pan. Bake at 350 degrees for 15 minutes. Let
cool. Spread Crumb Topping over cake. Bake an additional 15 to
20 minutes. Cool. Sift powdered sugar on top. Makes 12 to
16 servings.

Crumb Topping:

3 c. all-purpose flour
1/2 c. powdered sugar
1/2 c. brown sugar, packed

2 T. cinnamon
1/2 c. butter, melted
1 T. vanilla extract

Mix together flour, sugars and cinnamon. Mix butter and vanilla; pour
into flour mixture. Stir until crumbly.

At dessert time, set out whipped
cream and shakers of cinnamon
and cocoa for coffee drinkers.
Tea drinkers will love a basket
of special teas with honey and
lemon slices. Grandma's desserts
deserve the very best!

Yummy Carrot Cake

Cindy Beach
Franklin, NY

My grandma made this cake every year for Thanksgiving dinner at her farm. Grandma has been gone over twenty years now, and I honor her memory by making her carrot cake for my family's holiday. My husband always wants this cake for his birthday too. This recipe is by far my most requested!

4 eggs, beaten
2 c. sugar
1-1/4 c. oil
3 c. carrots, peeled and grated
2 c. all-purpose flour

2 t. cinnamon
2 t. baking soda
1 t. salt
Optional: chopped walnuts

Combine eggs, sugar, oil and carrots in a large bowl, beating well after adding each ingredient. In a separate bowl, sift together remaining ingredients except walnuts. Add to egg mixture; beat well to make a thin batter. Pour into a greased and lightly floured Bundt® pan; bake at 325 degrees for 40 to 50 minutes. A greased 13"x9" baking pan may also be used; bake at 325 degrees for 30 to 35 minutes. Cool. Frost with Cream Cheese Frosting; sprinkle with walnuts, if desired. Makes 12 to 15 servings.

Cream Cheese Frosting:

8-oz. pkg. cream cheese,
   softened

1/2 c. butter, softened
16-oz. pkg. powdered sugar

Blend all ingredients together until smooth.

Garnish cakes, cupcakes or cookies in a jiffy...sprinkle powdered sugar or cocoa through a doily.

Strawberry Layer Cake

Steven Wilson
Chesterfield, VA

Spring was always a wonderful time of year growing up in North Carolina...it meant strawberry time. I remember going with Grandma to the strawberry farm to pick those huge, luscious red berries, often eating as many as we put in the basket! She always used some of the fresh berries to make one of her delicious cakes to take to the Sunday night church social.

6-oz. pkg. strawberry gelatin mix
1/2 c. hot water
18-1/2 oz. pkg. white cake mix

2 T. all-purpose flour
1 c. strawberries, hulled and chopped
4 eggs

In a large bowl, dissolve dry gelatin mix in hot water; cool. Add dry cake mix, flour and strawberries; mix well. Add eggs, one at a time, beating slightly after each one. Pour batter into 3 greased 8" round cake pans. Bake at 350 degrees for 20 minutes, until cake tests done. Cool; assemble cake layers with Strawberry Frosting. Serves 12.

Strawberry Frosting:

1/4 c. butter, softened
3-3/4 to 5 c. powdered sugar

1/3 c. strawberries, hulled and finely chopped

Blend butter and powdered sugar together, adding sugar to desired consistency. Add strawberries; blend thoroughly.

Stored on the counter under a cake dome, a cake will stay fresh for about three days...if it lasts that long!

My Grandma's Chocolate Cake

Regina Wood
Ava, MO

*Grandma always baked this scrumptious made-from-scratch cake
when we were coming to visit her.*

3 c. all-purpose flour
2 c. sugar
1/3 c. baking cocoa
1/2 t. salt
2 t. baking soda

1 t. vanilla extract
3/4 c. oil
2 T. vinegar
2 c. cold water

In a large bowl, mix together all ingredients in order given. Blend
well; pour into a greased 13"x9" baking pan. Bake at 350 degrees for
35 minutes, or until a toothpick tests clean. Cool; frost with Chocolate
Frosting. Serves 12.

Chocolate Frosting:

1/3 c. butter-flavored shortening
1/3 c. baking cocoa
2 c. powdered sugar

1-1/2 t. vanilla extract
2 T. milk

Combine all ingredients; blend until smooth.

Turn a tried & true cake recipe into yummy cupcakes...so pretty
to serve, such fun to eat! Fill greased muffin cups 2/3 full of
cake batter. Bake at 350 degrees until a toothpick tests
clean, about 18 to 20 minutes. Cool and frost.

Granny's Pound Cake

Vici Randolph
Gaffney, SC

My granny has made this pound cake all my life. She has changed it so many times with different flavors of extract...I don't know if we ever had the same kind twice! I can remember Granny fussing at me when I was little because I would pick the crunchy topping off the pound cakes she made. It is still my favorite part of the cake today.

1/2 c. butter, softened
1/2 c. shortening
3 c. sugar
5 eggs
3 c. cake flour

1/2 t. baking powder
1 c. milk
2 t. vanilla, lemon or almond
   extract

Blend together butter, shortening and sugar. Add eggs, one at a time; beat well after each. In a separate bowl, sift together flour and baking powder. Add flour mixture to butter mixture, alternating with milk. Beat well; stir in extract. Pour batter into a greased 9" Bundt® pan. Place pan in a cold oven. Set to 325 degrees and bake for about 2 hours, or until a toothpick inserted in center tests clean. Makes 20 to 25 servings.

After dessert, take everyone on a nature hike at a nearby park or around the neighborhood. Take along a pocket-size nature guide, a magnifying glass and a tote bag to bring back special finds. Fun for young & old, and a great way to lose that too-full feeling!

Chip Apple Cake

Patty Scharinger
Leavenworth, KS

The sweet smell of Great-Grandma Harnish's Chip Apple Cake baking brings back many warm memories. I remember our entire family piling in the back of Grandpa's old truck to gather black walnuts, then coming back to Grandma's chicken & noodles or Grandpa's secret-recipe chili. Dessert, of course, would be Chip Apple Cake. When my youngest daughter was eight, she entered this cake in the county fair and was awarded reserve champion. I'm not sure who was proudest, Elizabeth, Grandma or myself!

2 c. Jonathan apples, cored,
    peeled and chopped
1 c. sugar
1/4 c. butter, melted
1 egg, beaten
1-1/2 c. all-purpose flour

1 t. baking soda
1/4 t. salt
1 t. cinnamon
Optional: 1/2 c. chopped
    walnuts

Toss together apples and sugar; let stand for 10 minutes. Drizzle melted butter over apples. Add egg; mix well and set aside. In a separate bowl, sift together flour, baking soda, salt and cinnamon. Add flour mixture to apple mixture; blend together. Stir in walnuts, if desired. Pour into a greased 8"x8" baking pan. Bake at 350 degrees for 40 minutes, or until a toothpick tests done. Makes 9 servings.

Any aspiring young baker would love to have his or her very own baking tools. Fill an unbreakable batter bowl with a wire whisk, measuring cups & spoons, an oven mitt and of course a cookbook...a gift that's sure to please!

Granny's Chocolate Cobbler

Lorrie Smith
Drummonds, TN

This recipe has been passed around in my family for years. It's just too yummy for words...yet oh-so quick & easy to make!

3/4 c. butter, melted
3 c. sugar, divided
1-1/2 c. self-rising flour
1/2 c. milk

1/2 c. plus 2 T. baking cocoa, divided
2 t. vanilla extract
2-1/2 c. boiling water

Spread melted butter in a 13"x9" baking pan; set aside. In a large bowl, combine 1-1/2 cups sugar, flour, milk, 2 tablespoons cocoa and vanilla. Pour over melted butter in pan. In a small bowl, mix together remaining sugar and cocoa; sprinkle evenly over batter. Pour boiling water over batter; do not stir. Bake at 350 degrees for 30 minutes. Serve warm. Makes 6 to 8 servings.

Fill a big apothecary jar with an assortment of retro penny candy...gumdrops, root beer barrels, caramels, sour balls, peppermints and lemon drops. Invite each guest to choose a favorite...such fun!

Grandma's Baked Apples

Rebecca Geyer
Bremen, IN

When I was a little girl, I had to wait until Thanksgiving to enjoy
Grandma Romaine's Baked Apples. Now that I have her recipe,
we make them year 'round...they're scrumptious!

8 to 12 Cortland apples, cored,
    peeled and sliced
1 c. brown sugar, packed
1/3 c. corn syrup
1/4 c. water

3 T. butter, sliced
1/3 c. all-purpose flour
cinnamon to taste
Garnish: sweetened whipped
    cream

To a greased 13"x9" baking pan, add water to 1/4-inch depth.
Arrange apple slices in pan. Bake, uncovered, at 375 degrees for
30 minutes. Drain; arrange apples evenly in pan and set aside. In a
saucepan over medium-low heat, combine brown sugar, corn syrup,
1/4 cup water, butter and flour. Cook and stir until thickened; spoon
over apples. Sprinkle apples with cinnamon. Bake at 350 degrees for
an additional 15 to 20 minutes. Serve warm with whipped cream.
Makes 12 servings.

Any homemade dessert is extra special topped with dollops of
whipped cream. It's oh-so simple too. In a chilled bowl,
with chilled beaters, whip a cup of whipping cream until soft
peaks form. Mix in 2 teaspoons sugar and 2 teaspoons
vanilla extract...and enjoy!

Country Rhubarb Crunch

Terri Clark
Huber Heights, OH

My grandma made this for all of us back in the 1950s and 1960s.
Our grandpa loved rhubarb and after Grandma found this recipe,
we loved it too. We still enjoy it and even the little ones like it.

1 c. plus 2 T. all-purpose flour,
    divided
2 c. sugar, divided
1 T. butter, diced
4 c. rhubarb, sliced

1 t. baking powder
1/4 t. salt
1 egg, beaten
Garnish: vanilla ice cream

In a large bowl, mix together 2 tablespoons flour, one cup sugar, butter and rhubarb. Spoon into an ungreased 8"x8" baking pan. In a separate bowl, mix together remaining flour, sugar, baking powder and salt. Add egg; mix. Mixture will be crumbly. Sprinkle over rhubarb mixture; shake pan so crumbs settle into rhubarb. Bake at 350 degrees for 40 minutes, or until crust is lightly golden. Serve warm or cold, topped with scoops of vanilla ice cream. Makes 8 servings.

Invite family & friends to a Sunday afternoon dessert social!
Everyone brings a pie, a cake or another favorite dessert...you
provide the ice cream and whipped topping.

Estelle's Baked Custard

Sharon Jones
Oklahoma City, OK

My Grandmother Estelle made this custard for as long as I can remember and now the secret has been passed down to me. It is one of my favorites...if you are a custard lover, you will love it too!

6 eggs
6 c. milk
1/2 c. sugar

1-1/2 t. vanilla extract
1/8 t. salt
Garnish: cinnamon or nutmeg

In a large bowl, whisk eggs until well beaten. Add milk, sugar, vanilla and salt; whisk well. Pour into 6 to 8 ungreased custard cups. Set cups in a rimmed baking pan. Pour an inch of hot water into baking pan. Bake at 325 degrees for one hour, or until a knife tip inserted in center tests clean. Sprinkle with cinnamon or nutmeg. Cool at room temperature or in refrigerator before serving, 1-1/2 to 2 hours. Serves 6 to 8.

Keep apple pie spice on hand to use in all kinds of desserts. A blend of cinnamon, nutmeg and allspice, it's like a spice rack in a bottle!

Princess Charlotte Pudding

Tracy Long
Bellwood, NE

This not-too-rich, pudding-like dessert always makes me think of Sunday dinners at my grandmother's house. My brother actually requests this instead of cake for his birthday!

2 c. milk, divided
1/2 c. sugar
1 T. cornstarch
2 eggs, beaten
1/2 t. vanilla extract

1 env. unflavored gelatin
1/4 c. hot water
8-oz. container frozen whipped
   topping, thawed
Optional: fresh berries

Whisk together milk, sugar and cornstarch until smooth. Add eggs; mix well. In a double boiler over medium heat, cook and stir mixture until thickened enough to coat a spoon. Remove from heat; cool to room temperature. In a cup, add gelatin to hot water; stir until dissolved. Stir into milk mixture until it begins to set; fold in whipped topping. Pour into a 13"x9" baking pan; cover and chill until set. Cut into squares; serve with Raspberry Sauce or fresh berries. Makes 12 servings.

Raspberry Sauce:

2 10-oz. pkgs. frozen
   raspberries, thawed

1 T. cornstarch

Strain seeds from berries by pushing through a sieve. Combine berries and cornstarch in a saucepan over medium-high heat. Bring to a boil. Cook, stirring frequently, until thickened slightly. Cool.

Happiness being a dessert so sweet,
May life give you more than you can ever eat.

-Irish toast

Farmhouse Blackberry Flummery

Ruth Donhauser
Somerville, NJ

I always loved my Grandma Stout's stories about her family's farm in Plainsboro, New Jersey. She spoke often of her own Grandma Britton making big lunches and desserts for her family and the farmhands... "Imagine cooking and baking while wearing those long dresses in those hot kitchens!" Blackberries were plentiful, and a flummery was a nice light fruit custard for summer days...it still is!

2 c. blackberries
3-1/2 c. water, divided
3/4 c. sugar
1/4 c. cornstarch

1/8 t. salt
juice of 1/2 lemon
Garnish: whipping cream or
  sour cream

In a large saucepan over low heat, simmer berries in one cup water for 5 minutes; drain. Return berries to saucepan; add remaining water. In a bowl, combine sugar, cornstarch and salt; add to berries. Cook over medium heat, stirring constantly until mixture thickens. Remove from heat; stir in lemon juice. Cool, stirring occasionally. Cover and chill; garnish as desired. Serves 4.

Garnish desserts with a strawberry fan...so pretty! Starting
at the tip, cut a strawberry into thin slices almost to the stem.
Carefully spread slices to form a fan.

Clara Mae's Peach Dessert

Robin Walters
Utica, MS

My grandmother received this cool, refreshing recipe from my Great-Aunt Clara Mae. We would enjoy it on hot summer days here in Mississippi. They are no longer with us, but whenever I make this dessert it brings back many happy memories.

6-oz. pkg. peach gelatin mix
2 c. boiling water
21-oz. can peach pie filling
15-1/4 oz. can crushed
   pineapple, drained
8-oz. pkg. cream cheese,
   softened

8-oz. container sour cream
1/4 c. sugar
1/4 c. powdered sugar
1 t. vanilla extract
1/2 c. shredded Cheddar cheese

In a large bowl, combine dry gelatin mix and boiling water. Stir for about 2 minutes, until dissolved. Add pie filling and pineapple; blend well. Pour into a 13"x9" baking pan. Cover and refrigerate until firm, about 4 hours. Combine remaining ingredients except shredded cheese in a separate bowl; beat with an electric mixer on medium-low speed until well blended. Spread over gelatin mixture; sprinkle shredded cheese on top. Cover and refrigerate until serving time. Cut into squares to serve. Serves 8.

Paper napkins that are anything but plain...just roll,
slip in plastic tableware and tie up with a
cheery gingham ribbon.

Homemade Banana Pudding

Traci Rodgers
Gas City, IN

My grandma was the cook at a small country school. She would make this dessert for the students and for family gatherings...it was a favorite for all. I think you'll love it too!

2 eggs, beaten
2 c. milk
1-1/2 c. brown sugar, packed
2 T. all-purpose flour
2 T. creamy or crunchy peanut
   butter

1 t. vanilla extract
1 to 2 bananas, sliced and
   divided
Optional: chopped peanuts

Whisk eggs and milk together in a bowl; set aside. In a saucepan, mix together brown sugar and flour. Add egg mixture to brown sugar mixture. Cook over medium-low heat, stirring constantly, until thickened. Add peanut butter and vanilla; whisk until creamy. Cool; transfer to a serving bowl. Fold banana slices into pudding, reserving a few slices for top of pudding. Garnish with reserved banana slices and sprinkle with peanuts, if desired. Makes 6 servings.

Spoon juicy fresh strawberries, blueberries or sliced nectarines into footed dessert dishes. Dollop with creamy vanilla yogurt for a heavenly light dessert...so welcome after a hearty meal.

SCRUMPTIOUS Desserts

Sweet Grape Delight

Lindsay Harter
Fort Atkinson, WI

My grandmother always made this creamy dessert for family gatherings. She received the recipe from her mother-in-law. Since it needs to be chilled, it's a great make-ahead for potlucks and socials.

8-oz. pkg. cream cheese, softened
8-oz. container sour cream
8-oz. container frozen whipped topping, thawed

1 lb. seedless green grapes
1 lb. seedless red grapes
1/2 to 1 c. chopped walnuts or pecans
1/2 c. brown sugar, packed

In a large bowl, mix together cream cheese, sour cream and whipped topping until well blended. Place grapes in a 13"x9" baking pan. Spoon cream cheese mixture over grapes. Mix together nuts and brown sugar; sprinkle on top. Cover and chill before serving. Makes 10 to 12 servings.

Ask Grandma to spend an afternoon showing you how to make the yummy dessert she's always been known for! Be sure to have a pad & pen handy so you can write down every step. When it's done, sample the dessert together along with cups of steamy hot tea or coffee.

Sunday Cake

April Hale
Kirkwood, NY

This recipe makes a lovely cake to serve with
coffee & tea after Sunday services.

1 c. butter of faith...to make life run smoothly
1 c. sugar...life needs its sweetness
5 eggs...to make it light...this is prayer, which uplifts
1/2 lb. nuts...humor...be sure they are clean!
1/4 lb. cherries...color the cake like music on a dull
    morning
1 lb. dates...are old friends, always a delight
1 lb. currants...are new friends, always interesting
1/4 t. allspice...puts tang in it like initiative
1/4 t. cinnamon...is ambition
2 t. baking powder to make it rise...this is the Holy Spirit
1/2 c. pure fresh milk...the perfect food which is the
    Word of God
1/2 t. salt...called wisdom
3 c. all-purpose flour...finely sifted to hold the whole cake
    together...just as love blends all life into one

In a large bowl, mix together all ingredients. Put in a greased 13"x9" baking pan. Bake in the slow oven of experience at

350 degrees for 45 to 60 minutes, until a cake tester comes out clean. When done, allow to cool. Add frosting to surround it with beauty and candles to light for all to see. Slice cake and share with others. Makes 12 servings.

HOMEMADE
Cookies
&
Candy

Beacon Hill Cookies

Jodi Hopkins
Everett, WA

My Great-Grandma Ann was a remarkable woman who lived to be 104. She credited that to her good Swedish genes as well as "never eating anything from a box." These cookies were one of my favorites. After she died, I asked my grandma if she had the recipe...I was so pleased that we found it, in Great-Grandma's handwriting!

1 c. butter, softened
1 c. sugar
2 egg yolks
1 t. vanilla extract
1-1/2 c. all-purpose flour

1/4 t. baking powder
1/8 t. salt
3/4 c. long-cooking oats,
   uncooked
3/4 c. crispy rice cereal

In a large bowl, blend all ingredients. Roll into one-inch balls; arrange on greased baking sheets. Press cookies with a fork, making a criss-cross shape. Bake at 375 degrees for 10 minutes, or until golden. Makes 3 dozen.

Search Grandma's recipe box for that extra-special cookie you remember...and then bake some to share with the whole family. If you don't have her recipe box, maybe you'll spot a similar recipe in a **Gooseberry Patch** cookbook!

Grandma's Hermits

Glenda Mitchell
Darrington, WA

My grandma baked these cookies for me when I was little, back in the 1950s. I always got to mix the shortening, sugar and eggs together and help put them on the baking sheet. At the ripe old age of five years, I really thought I was a great cook! She's gone now, but the spicy smell of Hermits baking always reminds me of her.

1 c. shortening
1-1/2 c. sugar
3 eggs, beaten
1/2 t. baking soda
2 t. water
3 c. all-purpose flour
1-1/2 t. salt

1 t. cinnamon
1 t. allspice
1 t. nutmeg
1 t. ground cloves
1-1/2 c. raisins
1/2 c. chopped nuts

In a large bowl, blend together shortening, sugar and eggs; set aside. In a cup, dissolve baking soda in water; add to shortening mixture. In a separate bowl, sift together flour, salt and spices; add to shortening mixture and mix well. Fold in raisins and nuts. Drop by teaspoonfuls onto greased baking sheets. Bake at 350 degrees for 15 to 20 minutes. Makes about 6 dozen.

Be sure to pull out the camera on baking day! Snapshots of children's little hands cutting out cookies, sweet faces smudged with frosting and gorgeous platters of decorated cookies are sure to be cherished for years to come.

Jubilee Jumbles

Holly Hansen
Tetonia, ID

My grandma made these cookies with their yummy glaze every Christmas. They were my dad's favorite growing up as a kid, and we so looked forward to them too. Grandma is no longer with us, but she lives on in our hearts with this recipe.

1/2 c. shortening
1 c. brown sugar, packed
1/2 c. sugar
2 eggs, beaten
1 c. evaporated milk

1 t. vanilla extract
2-3/4 c. all-purpose flour
1/2 t. baking soda
1 t. salt
Optional: 1/2 c. chopped nuts

In a large bowl, blend together shortening, sugars and eggs. Stir in evaporated milk and vanilla. In a separate bowl, sift together flour, baking soda and salt; stir into shortening mixture. Fold in nuts, if desired. Cover; chill dough for one hour. Drop by rounded teaspoonfuls onto baking sheets sprayed lightly with non-stick vegetable spray. Bake at 375 degrees for 10 minutes. Frost warm cookies with Burnt Butter Glaze. Makes 2-1/2 dozen.

Burnt Butter Glaze:

1/4 c. butter
2 c. powdered sugar

1/4 c. evaporated milk

In a saucepan over medium heat, cook butter until dark golden. Remove from heat. Beat in remaining ingredients until smooth.

Borrow Grandma's secret for keeping cookies moist...slip a slice of bread into the cookie jar!

Soft Chocolate Chip Cookies

Melody Foutty
Geary, OK

My mom always made these quick & easy
cookies...everyone loved them!

18-1/2 oz. pkg. white cake mix
1/2 c. oil
2 T. water

2 eggs, beaten
1 c. semi-sweet chocolate chips
1/2 c. chopped nuts

In a large bowl, mix together dry cake mix, oil, water and eggs. Stir in chocolate chips and nuts. Drop by teaspoonfuls onto ungreased baking sheets. Bake at 350 degrees for 12 minutes, or until golden. Makes 3 to 4 dozen.

Once in a young lifetime, one should be allowed to have as much sweetness as one can possibly want and hold.

-Judith Olney

Baba's Favorites

Louise Maksymetz
Manitoba, Canada

This recipe was given to my mother by her mother, whom we called Baba. When I was twelve, we went to visit my grandparents on their farm. I brought them these wonderful cookies which I had baked from my grandmother's own recipe. Baba was thrilled that I would bake for her and I was delighted to do it. Such memories!

3/4 c. shortening
1 c. brown sugar, packed
1/2 c. sugar
2 eggs
1/4 c. milk
2-1/4 c. all-purpose flour
1 t. baking soda

1 t. salt
1-1/2 t. cinnamon
1/2 t. nutmeg
3 c. long-cooking oats, uncooked
1 c. raisins, chopped
Garnish: sugar

In a large bowl, beat shortening and sugars until creamy. Add eggs, one at a time, beating after each one. Add milk, beating until well blended and smooth; set aside. In a separate bowl, sift together flour, baking soda, salt and spices. Add flour mixture to shortening mixture; blend together. Fold in oats and raisins. Cover; refrigerate dough for one hour. Roll out to 1/4-inch thick on a lightly floured board. Cut with a floured 3-inch round cookie cutter. Place on greased baking sheets; sprinkle with sugar. Bake at 375 degrees for 10 to 12 minutes. Makes 3 dozen.

Découpage a copy of Grandma's favorite cookie recipe onto the lid of a tin...such a sweet keepsake!

Georgia's Buttermilk-Orange Cookies
Marge Wearing
Renfrew, PA

Grandma Georgia Marburger was well-known in the small town of Evans City, Pennsylvania. The dairy she started in 1938 with her husband Adam, is still family owned and operated. My dad, who was her oldest son, still checks on the dairy every day at the age of ninety-two.

1 c. butter, softened	1 t. baking powder
2 c. sugar	1 t. baking soda
2 eggs, beaten	1 c. buttermilk
4-1/2 c. all-purpose flour	zest and juice of 1 orange

Blend together butter and sugar in a large bowl. Add eggs and beat well. In a separate bowl, sift together flour, baking powder and baking soda. Add flour mixture to butter mixture alternately with buttermilk; mix well. Stir in zest and juice. Drop by tablespoonfuls onto lightly greased baking sheets. Bake at 350 degrees for 8 to 12 minutes. Cool cookies completely before frosting. Makes 4 dozen.

Frosting:

4 c. powdered sugar	juice of 1/2 orange
2 T. butter, melted	

Blend ingredients together in a small bowl until smooth.

There's no place like Grandma's

Delectable Date-Nut Cookies

Shannon Bishop
Kingsport, TN

My great-grandmother always kept these sweet date-filled cookies in her freezer for when company would drop by. You couldn't leave her house without taking home a care package of these cookies!

1 c. margarine, softened
2 c. brown sugar, packed
3 eggs, beaten

4 c. all-purpose flour
1 t. baking soda
1/8 t. salt

Blend together margarine and brown sugar. Add remaining ingredients; mix well. Cover and chill dough for one hour; divide into 4 parts. Roll out each part 1/2-inch thick on a floured surface. Spread with Date Filling; roll up jelly-roll fashion. Chill again. Slice 1/4-inch thick; place on lightly greased baking sheets. Bake at 400 degrees for 12 minutes. Makes 2 dozen.

Date Filling:

1 lb. dates, chopped
1/2 c. water

1/2 c. sugar
1/2 c. black walnuts, chopped

In a saucepan over medium-low heat, combine dates, water and sugar. Cook 5 minutes, stirring frequently. Add walnuts; cool.

For best results when baking cookies, set out butter and eggs on the kitchen counter an hour ahead of time, so they can come to room temperature.

Mama's Colonial Cookies

Diane Price
Nappanee, IN

My parents' front door was always open to family & friends.
Mom kept her cookie jar filled with her yummy cookies...this is one
recipe that I fondly remember.

1 c. sugar
1 c. brown sugar, packed
1 c. lard or shortening
2 eggs, beaten
2 t. vanilla extract
2 c. all-purpose flour
1 t. baking powder

1 t. baking soda
1 t. salt
2 c. quick-cooking oats,
  uncooked
1-1/2 c. sweetened flaked
  coconut
1-1/2 c. chopped pecans

In a large bowl, beat together sugars and lard or shortening until
creamy. Add eggs and vanilla; mix well. In a separate bowl, sift
together flour, baking powder, baking soda and salt. Add flour mixture
to sugar mixture; blend well. Add oats, coconut and pecans; mix with
hands. Drop by heaping tablespoonfuls onto ungreased non-stick
baking sheets. Bake at 350 degrees for 10 minutes, or until golden.
Makes about 3 dozen.

Serve up warm, fresh-baked cookies at a moment's notice. Roll
dough into cookie-size balls and freeze to share later...remember
to tuck in a card with the recipe name and baking instructions.
Balls of frozen dough can go directly onto baking sheets,
no thawing required.

German Anise Cookies

Colleen Busch
Alliance, NE

Several years ago, when my parents came out for the holidays I was doing my Christmas baking. After trying one of the anise roll-out cookies I'd made, Mom recalled that her mom used to make anise drop cookies when she was a girl and she hadn't had them in a very long time. I asked Grandma if she knew what cookie I was taking about... thank heavens she did! Grandma shared the recipe with me...now these cookies are a family tradition.

2 eggs, room temperature
1 c. sugar

3/4 t. anise extract
1 c. all-purpose flour

Place eggs in a large bowl. Beat with an electric mixer on high speed for 4 minutes. Gradually beat in sugar. Continue beating on high speed for 10 minutes, until mixture thickens. Add extract; reduce mixer to low speed and beat in flour. Drop dough by rounded teaspoonfuls onto greased baking sheets. Let dry at room temperature, 10 to 12 hours or overnight. Do not refrigerate. Bake on top rack of oven at 350 degrees for 10 to 12 minutes. Remove cookies from baking sheets as soon as they come out of oven. Makes 2 to 2-1/2 dozen.

Parchment paper is a baker's best friend. Place it on a baking sheet to keep cookies from spreading and sticking. Clean-up is a breeze too...just toss away the paper! You'll find rolls of parchment paper in the grocery store, next to wax paper.

Coconut Macaroons

Vickie

*An old-fashioned treat...we just love these sweet,
chewy little morsels of coconut.*

4 egg whites, beaten
1 t. vanilla extract
1/8 t. almond extract

3/4 c. sugar
1/4 t. salt
3 c. sweetened flaked coconut

In a large bowl, whisk together all ingredients except coconut. Add
coconut; mix well. Drop by rounded teaspoonfuls onto parchment
paper-lined baking sheets. Bake at 325 degrees for about 25 minutes,
or until set and golden; rotate baking sheets between upper and lower
oven racks halfway through baking time. Cool on baking sheets for
one minute; transfer to wire racks and cool completely. Store in an
airtight container. Makes about 3-1/2 dozen.

Try sugar-substitute blends made especially for baking
to turn out sweet, golden, moist goodies with half the sugar.
There's even a brown sugar variety! Be sure to check
the package for how to measure correctly.

Old-Time Molasses Cookies

Alysson Marshall
Newark, NY

Whenever we stopped to visit my Grandma Hoak, she had a plate of molasses cookies ready to serve along with a glass of milk or a cup of tea. These days she doesn't bake much anymore, but I can still remember the sweet scent of these cookies in her cozy home along with her welcoming hugs.

3/4 c. shortening
2 c. powdered sugar
1 c. molasses
1 egg, beaten
4 c. all-purpose flour
2 t. baking soda

1 t. salt
1 t. cinnamon
2 t. ground ginger
1 t. vanilla extract
Garnish: powdered sugar

In a large bowl, blend together shortening, powdered sugar, molasses and egg. Add remaining ingredients except garnish; stir until blended. Roll into one-inch balls and place on ungreased baking sheets. Bake at 350 degrees for 10 to 12 minutes, until cookies crack. Cool; dip tops in powdered sugar. Makes 5 dozen.

Grandma always said, "Never return a dish empty."
Gather up cookie tins, pie plates and casserole dishes that
have been left behind, fill them with homebaked goodies and
return them to their owners...they'll be pleasantly surprised!

Grandma's Vanilla Horns

Charlene Blackburn
Mapleton, KS

These crunchy almond cookies can be made ahead of time and kept in a cookie tin for several weeks. Here's Grandma's little trick...soak a folded paper towel with vanilla extract, place it in a small plastic bag and tuck the unsealed bag into the tin on top of the cookies.

1 lb. butter, softened
1 c. sugar
2 t. vanilla extract

1 c. almonds, finely chopped
3 c. all-purpose flour
Garnish: powdered sugar

Blend together butter and sugar in a large bowl; stir in vanilla and almonds. Gradually add flour until dough can be shaped with your hands. Cover; refrigerate dough for one hour. Form into crescent shapes, about 1/2-inch thick and 2 inches long. Place on ungreased baking sheets. Bake at 350 degrees for about 15 minutes, or until golden. Remove from oven; cool slightly, then roll in powdered sugar to coat. Store in a covered container. Makes about 3 dozen.

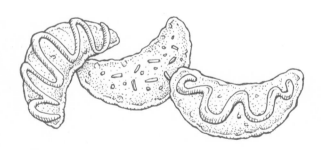

Show little ones you love 'em...give 'em hugs & kisses!
Roll cookie dough into ropes and form X's and O's on a baking sheet. Sprinkle with sparkling sugar before baking...so sweet!

Brown Sugar Cut-Outs

Sherry Berresford
Kensington, OH

*My Grandmother Kaser's sugar cookie recipe has been enjoyed
for the past six generations...that's a lot of cookies!*

1 c. margarine, softened
2 c. brown sugar, packed
2 eggs, beaten
4-1/2 c. all-purpose flour
2 t. baking powder

1 t. baking soda
1/2 c. milk
1 t. vanilla extract
1 t. lemon extract
Optional: sugar or frosting

In a large bowl, combine all ingredients except optional ingredients; mix well. Cover; refrigerate for one hour. Roll out dough 1/2-inch thick on a floured surface. Cut out shapes with cookie cutters. Place cookies one inch apart on greased and floured baking sheets. If desired, sprinkle cookies with sugar. Bake at 350 degrees for 10 minutes, or until golden around edges. Cool for one minute before removing from baking sheets; cool completely on wax paper. Decorate cooled cookies with frosting, if preferred. Makes about 4 dozen.

Create a cookie bouquet for an edible centerpiece. Fill a terra-cotta pot with florists' foam that's been cut to fit inside; cover the foam with moss. Place flower-shaped decorated cookies on wooden skewers and tuck the skewers into the foam.

Raisin Rocks

Carolyn Britton
Millry, AL

My grandmother always made these spicy fruit & nut cookies for the holidays...they went perfectly with her ambrosia salad.

1-1/2 c. brown sugar, packed
2/3 c. butter-flavored shortening
2 eggs
1 t. vanilla extract
2-1/2 c. all-purpose flour
1 t. baking soda
1/4 t. salt
1 t. cinnamon
1/4 t. ground cloves
3 c. chopped pecans
1-1/2 c. raisins

In a large bowl, blend together brown sugar and shortening until light and fluffy. Add eggs one at a time; beat well after each. Stir in vanilla; set aside. In a separate bowl, sift together dry ingredients. Gradually add flour mixture to brown sugar mixture; mix well. Fold in pecans and raisins. Drop by teaspoonfuls onto parchment paper-lined baking sheets. Bake at 325 degrees for 10 to 15 minutes, until golden. Makes 6 dozen.

For plump, juicy raisins, cover them with boiling water and let stand for 15 minutes. Drain and pat dry with a paper towel before adding to your cookie recipe.

Chocolate Overnight Cookies

Becky Morris
Aberdeen, SD

These cookies are really good dunked in milk or coffee. I remember my Grandma Marcy making these...I would sneak into the fridge to eat the dough before she'd had a chance to bake them. I don't really recommend doing that anymore!

2-1/2 c. all-purpose flour
1/4 t. baking soda
3/4 c. butter, softened
1 c. sugar
1 egg, beaten

1 t. vanilla extract
1 T. milk
3 sqs. unsweetened baking
   chocolate, melted
1/2 c. chopped walnuts

In a medium bowl, mix flour and baking soda; set aside. In a large bowl, blend remaining ingredients in order given. Add flour mixture to butter mixture; mix well. Form dough into a log about 2 inches in diameter and wrap in wax paper. Refrigerate overnight. Slice dough 1/8-inch thick; place on ungreased baking sheets. Bake at 400 degrees for 6 to 8 minutes. Makes about 3 dozen.

Host a cookie sampling party! Have each friend bring a plate of her very best cookies, while you provide the coffee and tea. Vote on the tastiest, most beautiful and cleverest cookies...hand out ribbons or little prizes. What fun!

Butterscotch Icebox Cookies

Cathy Jepson
Modesto, CA

My grandmother used to make these cookies. They are still my favorite...so easy to make and so good to eat. Be sure to start a day ahead so the dough can chill overnight.

1 c. butter, softened	4 c. all-purpose flour
2 c. brown sugar, packed	1 t. baking soda
2 eggs	1 t. cream of tartar
1 t. vanilla extract	1 c. chopped walnuts

In a large bowl, blend together butter and brown sugar until light. Add eggs, one at a time, mixing thoroughly. Stir in vanilla. Add dry ingredients and nuts; mix well. Form into 2 logs; wrap in wax paper, then in aluminum foil. Refrigerate overnight. Slice dough 1/4-inch thick; place on ungreased baking sheets. Bake at 350 degrees for 10 to 12 minutes. Makes about 4 dozen.

A take-home favor that's sure to be appreciated! Pack chunky, chewy cookies in clear cellophane bags...fold the top over and make two holes with a hole punch. Thread a ribbon through the holes and tie it in a bow...how clever!

Hannah's Lemon Bars

Tina George
El Dorado, AR

My family just loves these sweet-tart lemon bars, especially my daughter, Hannah. When she's having an extra-busy day of college and work, I'll make a batch just for her...they perk her right up!

1-1/2 c. plus 3 T. all-purpose
    flour, divided
1 c. powdered sugar, divided
3/4 c. butter, softened

3 eggs, beaten
1-1/2 c. sugar
1/4 c. lemon juice

In a large bowl, combine 1-1/2 cups flour, 2/3 cup powdered sugar and butter. Mix well; pat into a greased 13"x9" baking pan. Bake at 350 degrees for 20 minutes; remove from oven. Whisk eggs, sugar, remaining flour and lemon juice together until frothy; pour over hot crust. Bake at 350 degrees for 20 to 25 minutes, until light golden. Cool in pan on a wire rack. Dust with remaining powdered sugar. Cut into bars. Makes 3 to 4 dozen.

At tag sales and flea markets, keep an eye out for vintage cookie cutters. With their one-of-a-kind shapes, they're sure to add lots of whimsy to cut-out cookies.

Pineapple-Raisin Cookies

Linda Crandall
Sandy Creek, NY

I think of my grandma every time I bake these cookies...she knew how much I loved them!

1/2 c. shortening, melted and
    slightly cooled
1 c. brown sugar, packed
1 egg, beaten
1/2 t. vanilla extract
2 c. all-purpose flour

1/2 t. baking powder
1/2 t. baking soda
1/2 t. salt
1/2 c. crushed pineapple,
    drained
1/2 c. raisins

In a large bowl, blend shortening and brown sugar together; stir in egg and vanilla. In a separate bowl, mix together flour, baking powder, baking soda and salt. Add flour mixture to shortening mixture; mix well. Stir in pineapple and raisins. Drop by tablespoonfuls onto greased baking sheets. Bake at 375 degrees for 12 minutes. Makes 3 dozen.

A fast and fun party punch to serve with cookies. Simply combine a 2-liter bottle of chilled soda with a pint of sherbet. Match up flavors...strawberry sherbet with strawberry soda, rainbow sherbet with lemon-lime soda. Yummy!

Granny's Tea Cake Cookies

Paula Trotti Patrick
Kathleen, GA

As a child, I can remember watching my granny and my great-grandmother making these cookies together...laughing, talking and just catching up on each other's lives as they worked. When I got older, the picture changed and then it was Granny, my mother and me spending time together making cookies. When my boys were younger, we spent hours making cookies too. There are many wonderful memories in this recipe!

1 c. shortening
2-1/2 c. sugar
3 eggs, beaten
1 t. vanilla extract

4 t. buttermilk
3 c. all-purpose flour
1 t. baking soda

In a large bowl, blend shortening and sugar. Add remaining ingredients; beat until dough is sticky. Spoon onto wax paper; wrap and refrigerate for several hours to overnight. Roll out dough 1/2-inch thick on a floured surface. Cut out shapes with floured cookie cutters; transfer to greased baking sheets. Bake at 350 degrees for 8 to 10 minutes, until edges are golden. Makes about 4 dozen.

Use a smaller cookie cutter to create a cut-out inside a cookie. Fill the cut-out with crushed hard candy before baking. As it bakes and melts, the candy magically creates a stained-glass look.

Melt-in-Your-Mouth Cookies

Anna Fischer
Ferdinand, IN

*When I was a child, my grandmother would always keep these cookies
on hand. To this day, they are still my favorite cookies.*

1/2 c. butter, softened
1 c. brown sugar, packed
1 egg, beaten
1 t. vanilla extract
3/4 c. all-purpose flour

1 t. salt
1 t. baking powder
1/2 c. chopped pecans or
   walnuts

In a medium bowl, blend together butter and brown sugar. Add egg
and vanilla; beat until light. Blend in remaining ingredients. Drop by
teaspoonfuls onto greased or parchment paper-lined baking sheets.
Bake at 375 degrees for 7 minutes, or until golden on the edges.
Makes 2 dozen.

After a farmhouse-size dinner, a simple dessert is perfect.
Enjoy assorted homemade cookies accompanied by
scoops of sherbet or fruit salad in footed dishes.

Favorite Gumdrop Cookies

Celeste Reszel
Des Moines, IA

This is my great-grandmother's cookie recipe...she always kept them in her freezer for when we came to visit!

1 c. shortening
1 c. sugar
1/2 c. brown sugar, packed
2 eggs, beaten
1 t. vanilla extract

2-1/3 c. all-purpose flour
1 t. baking soda
1 t. salt
1 c. gumdrops, chopped
Optional: 1/2 c. chopped nuts

In a large bowl, blend together shortening, sugars, eggs and vanilla. Add flour, baking soda and salt. Fold in gumdrops and nuts, if desired. Mix well. Drop by teaspoonfuls onto ungreased baking sheets. Bake at 350 degrees for 15 minutes. Makes about 4 dozen.

Use kitchen shears to make short work of cutting up gumdrops, dates and other sticky cookie ingredients.

Grandma Danielson's Soft Sugar Cookies

Lou Ann Peterson
Frewsburg, NY

At least five generations of my family have loved these cookies! Whenever it was our turn to bring treats to school, my brothers & I always asked to take Grandma's sugar cookies. Now my daughter, Sarah, and niece, Alyssa, make them too and I'm sure this recipe will continue to be handed down.

1 c. shortening
1-1/2 c. sugar
2 eggs, beaten
1 t. vanilla extract
1/2 c. milk
4 c. all-purpose flour

1-1/2 t. baking soda
1 t. baking powder
1/2 t. salt
Optional: frosting, colored sugar,
        candy sprinkles

Blend together shortening and sugar in a large bowl; add eggs and beat well. Add vanilla, milk and dry ingredients; mix together well. Roll out dough 1/4-inch to 1/2-inch thick on a floured surface. Cut out shapes with cookie cutters; transfer to lightly greased baking sheets. Bake at 350 degrees for about 10 minutes, or until cookies are golden on the bottom. Frost or decorate, if desired. Makes 4 to 6 dozen, depending on size of cookie cutters used.

When decorating with candy sprinkles, cover the table first with a length of wax paper. Return any excess sprinkles to their jars by simply folding the paper in half, gently shaking sprinkles to one side and sliding them into the jar.

Medallion Roll-Out Cookies

Mel Chencharick
Julian, PA

This recipe brings back such wonderful memories of three generations in my kitchen baking cookies together! It's great for using your favorite cookie cutters. I still have some of the old cookie cutters used by my grandmother and will hand them on to my granddaughter too.

2/3 c. shortening
1-1/2 c. sugar
2 eggs, beaten
1 t. vanilla extract

4 t. milk
3-1/3 c. all-purpose flour
2-1/2 t. baking powder
1/2 t. salt

In a large bowl, blend shortening and sugar; add eggs, vanilla and milk. In a separate bowl, mix remaining ingredients. Add flour mixture to shortening mixture; stir until well blended. Divide dough into 3 or 4 balls; wrap in plastic wrap and chill for at least one hour. Roll out dough 1/4-inch thick on a floured surface. Cut out shapes with cookie cutters. Transfer to ungreased baking sheets. Bake at 400 degrees for 7 to 9 minutes. Makes about 3 dozen.

For the tastiest cookies, use the type of fat that the recipe calls for...it's best not to substitute. Real butter bakes up well and gives cookies wonderful flavor. If shortening is called for, look for it in easy-to-measure sticks...it's fine to use the butter-flavored variety.

Sour Cream Drop Cookies

Cheryl Bastian
Northumberland, PA

This recipe was given to me by my grandmother.
The citrus extract makes it taste extra special.

3/4 c. butter, softened
1-1/2 c. sugar
2 eggs, beaten
1 t. vanilla extract
1/2 t. lemon or orange extract

8-oz. container sour cream
3 c. all-purpose flour
1 t. baking powder
1 t. baking soda

In a large bowl, blend together butter and sugar. Add eggs, vanilla and extract; mix well. Fold in sour cream; set aside. Combine remaining ingredients; gradually add to butter mixture. Drop by teaspoonfuls onto greased baking sheets. Bake at 350 degrees for 10 to 12 minutes. Makes 3 dozen.

A one-gallon glass apothecary jar makes a great cookie jar. Personalize it by using a glass paint pen to add a message like "Family Favorite Cookies" and hearts or swirls just for fun.

Mean Jean's Pumpkin Cookies

Natalie Anstine
Canton, OH

My granny "Mean Jean" used to make these scrumptious cookies and now I carry on the tradition. Despite her amusing nickname, she was always loving to us grandkids.

1-1/2 c. shortening
1 c. sugar
1 c. brown sugar, packed
2 eggs, beaten
1-1/2 c. canned pumpkin
1 t. vanilla extract

3-1/2 c. all-purpose flour
1/2 t. salt
1 t. baking soda
1 T. cinnamon
12-oz. pkg. butterscotch chips

In a large bowl, blend together shortening, sugars, eggs, pumpkin and vanilla. In a separate bowl, mix remaining ingredients except butterscotch chips. Gradually add flour mixture to shortening mixture, continuing to stir. Mix well; stir in butterscotch chips. Drop by tablespoonfuls onto ungreased baking sheets. Bake at 350 degrees for 11 to 13 minutes. Remove to wire racks. Frost when cool; let frosting dry completely before storing. Makes 3 to 4 dozen.

Powdered Sugar Frosting:

1/4 c. butter, melted
2-1/2 c. powdered sugar
1 t. vanilla extract

2 T. cream cheese, softened
1 to 2 T. milk

Mix all ingredients together until smooth, adding milk as needed.

Decorate a gift bag of treats in a jiffy...glue on a color copy of a vintage postcard featuring your hometown's name.

White Chocolate Cranberry Cookies

Lea Burwell
Charlestown, WV

This is a family favorite...even Grandma can't resist eating one of these mouthwatering cookies!

1/2 c. butter-flavored shortening
1/4 c. sugar
1 c. light brown sugar, packed
3.4-oz. pkg. instant French
  vanilla pudding mix
1/2 t. baking soda

1-1/2 t. vanilla extract
2-1/2 c. all-purpose flour
1-1/2 c. white chocolate chips
1/2 c. macadamia nuts, crushed
1 c. dried cranberries

In a large bowl, blend together shortening, sugars, dry pudding mix, baking soda, vanilla and flour. Fold in remaining ingredients. Drop by tablespoonfuls onto parchment-lined baking sheets. Bake at 375 degrees for 8 minutes. Makes about 3-1/2 dozen.

Wrapping up a care package of cookies to mail? How thoughtful! Choose sturdy cookies that won't crumble easily. Bar cookies, brownies and drop cookies are great travelers, while frosted or filled cookies may be too fragile.

Peanut Butter Brownies

Krysti Hilfiger
Covington, PA

My grandmother told me this quick & easy recipe came from my
great-great-grandmother...no wonder it's one of my favorites!

1/3 c. shortening
2 T. baking cocoa
1 c. sugar
2 eggs, beaten

1/2 c. all-purpose flour
1/4 t. salt
1/3 c. creamy peanut butter

In a small saucepan over low heat, melt shortening and cocoa
together. Cool; transfer to a medium bowl. Stir in sugar and eggs; add
flour and salt. Mix well; fold in peanut butter. Spread in a greased
8"x8" baking pan. Bake at 350 degrees for 20 to 25 minutes. Cool;
cut into squares. Makes one dozen.

For a chocolatey topping in a jiffy, sprinkle brownies or
bar cookies with chocolate chips as soon as they come out of
the oven. When chips soften, spread them with a spatula. Yum!

Martha's Brownie Bars

Teresa Jordan
Easley, SC

This recipe for brown sugar brownies was given to my grandmother by her friend, Martha. Our whole family loves them. They are so yummy...it's hard to eat just one!

3/4 c. butter
2 c. brown sugar, packed
3 eggs, beaten
1 t. vanilla extract

2 c. self-rising flour
Optional: 1 c. chopped pecans,
    whipped topping

Place butter in a 13"x9" baking pan; set in a 350-degree oven to melt; let cool slightly. Place brown sugar in a bowl; pour melted butter over brown sugar. Add eggs, vanilla, flour and nuts, if using; mix well and pour back into same baking pan. Bake at 350 degrees for 10 minutes. Reduce oven temperature to 325 degrees; bake for an additional 25 to 30 minutes. Cool completely; slice into bars. Top with whipped topping, if desired. Makes 1-1/2 to 2 dozen.

Invite a young friend to bake with you. Whether you're a basic baker or a master chef, you're sure to have fun as you measure, stir and sample together.

Grandma's Popcorn Balls

Andrea Ebersol
Gordonville, PA

When my grandma created a homemade cookbook in 1966, she included this recipe. These popcorn balls are a family tradition every fall...but they're fun any time of year!

20 c. popped popcorn
2 c. sugar
1/2 c. water

2/3 c. corn syrup
1 t. vanilla extract
1 t. salt

Place popcorn in a large heat-proof bowl; set aside. In a saucepan over medium heat, mix together remaining ingredients. Bring to a rolling boil. Stir mixture until it reaches the thread stage, or 230 to 233 degrees on a candy thermometer. Pour over popcorn; mix well and form into balls with well-buttered hands. Wrap balls in squares of wax paper. Makes about 10.

For your favorite college student who's away from home, a care package of sweets is a terrific surprise! Along with homemade goodies, tuck in a phone card and some family photos...so thoughtful!

Granny's Chocolate Fudge

Christy Bonner
Berry, AL

This is a family recipe that my granny passed down to me. She received this recipe from a dear friend of hers in El Paso, Texas, when my Papaw was serving in the war. It has never failed me and always turns out scrumptious.

4-1/2 c. sugar
1-1/2 c. margarine
12-oz. can evaporated milk
3 6-oz. pkgs. semi-sweet
   chocolate chips

1 t. vanilla extract
13-oz. jar marshmallow creme
2 c. chopped pecans or walnuts

In a large, heavy saucepan over medium-high heat, combine sugar, margarine and evaporated milk. Bring to a rolling boil; boil for 5 minutes, stirring constantly. Remove from heat; add remaining ingredients. Stir until smooth and chocolate is melted. Pour onto a greased 15"x10" jelly-roll pan. Let stand overnight, or until firm. Cut into one-inch squares. Makes 5 pounds.

A recipe for success...to ensure that homemade fudge
will set up properly, always make just one batch
at a time.

GG's Ladyfingers Candy

Carol Hickman
Kingsport, TN

My husband's grandmother GG, as she likes to be called, has always made this delicious candy for Christmas. Whenever visitors stop by, she pulls out a tin of candy for them to enjoy. For twenty-seven years she managed to avoid giving me the recipe, but last December my teenage daughter helped her make the candy. At the end of the day, GG sent home a copy of the recipe for me. That was the highlight of my holiday!

16-oz. pkg. powdered sugar
1 c. pecans or walnuts, finely
  chopped
2 c. sweetened flaked coconut
1 c. graham cracker crumbs
1 c. marshmallow creme

1 c. creamy peanut butter
1 t. vanilla extract
1 c. butter, melted
12-oz. pkg. semi-sweet
  chocolate chips
1/2 bar paraffin wax, chopped

In a large bowl, combine all ingredients except butter, chocolate chips and paraffin. Pour melted butter over mixture; stir to combine. Chill one to 2 hours. Form tablespoonfuls of mixture into "fingers" and place on wax paper-lined baking sheets. Chill an additional one to 2 hours. In the top of a double boiler, combine chocolate chips and paraffin over low heat. Stir until completely melted and smooth. With a fork, dip "fingers" into chocolate. Allow excess chocolate to drip back into pan; place on wax paper to cool. Keep refrigerated. Makes about 5 dozen.

Slice 'n Bake
Sugar Cookie Dough

Short on time? Why not pick up a tube of refrigerated cookie dough to bake with the kids. Add some candy sprinkles and ready-to-use frosting...it's all about making memories together!

INDEX

INDEX

Candy

Cookies

Mains

INDEX

Pickles & Preserves

Salads

Sides

Snacks

Soups

Have a taste for more?

We created our official Circle of Friends so we could
fill everyone in on the latest scoop at once.
Visit us online to join in the fun and discover free
recipes, exclusive giveaways and much more!

www.gooseberrypatch.com

 Join Our Circle of Friends

 Find Gooseberry Patch in Your Neighborhood

 Find us on Facebook

 You Tube

 Follow us on twitter

 Read Our Blog

Call us toll-free at 1·800·854·6673

U.S. to Canadian recipe equivalents

Volume Measurements

1/4 teaspoon	1 mL
1/2 teaspoon	2 mL
1 teaspoon	5 mL
1 tablespoon = 3 teaspoons	15 mL
2 tablespoons = 1 fluid ounce	30 mL
1/4 cup	60 mL
1/3 cup	75 mL
1/2 cup = 4 fluid ounces	125 mL
1 cup = 8 fluid ounces	250 mL
2 cups = 1 pint =16 fluid ounces	500 mL
4 cups = 1 quart	1 L

Weights

1 ounce	30 g
4 ounces	120 g
8 ounces	225 g
16 ounces = 1 pound	450 g

Oven Temperatures

300° F	150° C
325° F	160° C
350° F	180° C
375° F	190° C
400° F	200° C
450° F	230° C

Baking Pan Sizes

Square		
8x8x2 inches	2 L = 20x20x5 cm	
9x9x2 inches	2.5 L = 23x23x5 cm	
Rectangular		
13x9x2 inches	3.5 L = 33x23x5 cm	

Loaf		
9x5x3 inches	2 L = 23x13x7 cm	
Round		
8x1-1/2 inches	1.2 L = 20x4 cm	
9x1-1/2 inches	1.5 L = 23x4 cm	